WHILE ANGELS
WERE WATCHING

Wyvonnia Smith-Gorden

TRILOGY

Trilogy Christian Publishers
A Wholly Owned Subsidiary of Trinity Broadcasting Network
2442 Michelle Drive
Tustin, CA 92780

For information, address Trilogy Christian Publishing
Rights Department, 2442 Michelle Drive, Tustin, Ca 92780.
Trilogy Christian Publishing/ TBN and colophon are trademarks
of Trinity Broadcasting Network.
For information about special discounts for bulk purchases,
please contact Trilogy Christian Publishing.
Manufactured in the United States of America

10 9 8 7 6 5 4 3 2 1
Library of Congress Cataloging-in-Publication Data is available.
ISBN 978-1-64773-835-8
ISBN 978-1-64773-836-5 (ebook)

DEDICATION

This book is dedicated to my children, my siblings, Michele and Vincent (who encouraged me to write this book), and Ms. Catherine (now deceased), who was also my inspiration. I have included one of her poems that she wrote for me when I was having trials in life called "God's Amazing Grace."

I started this book years ago because it was healing for me to write down the things that were driving me, making me happy, or simply life situations over which I had no control. It has taken me a long time to complete it. My son has always encouraged me, but it was not until I met Michele that I finally realized that someone other than my son might be interested in what I had to say. Michele is one of those angels who appears in life and has influenced me in a way that only God could have done. She convinced me that what I had to say was of interest to more than just my children and should be shared with everyone.

So, to all of you: thanks for your love and support. Because of you, I am truly blessed!

TABLE OF CONTENTS

1.

THE EARLY YEARS OF MY LIFE
FROM MY HEART TO YOURS

"Shared stories build a relational bridge that Jesus can walk across from your heart to others."

Pastor Rick Warren

My greatest influence in life, as well as my greatest motivator, was my father (other than my father, it was Jesus Christ). My father's wisdom, love, care, and faith could not be overlooked in my life. He was the one that I called when I needed advice, or if I just needed a word of comfort. He was never too busy nor disinterested in whatever I wanted to talk about. He seemed to be there for me as well as the other siblings. I realized that it is hard to give a lot of individual attention to ten kids, but I am eternally grateful for the time, love, and guidance that he gave me. As you read these stories, you will better understand why, from my perspective, my father was the best.

He is the one who coined the term "Frank-isms," as his children so lovingly called them. These are sayings that I use on a regular basis, even to this day. I am sure that ten different children would have ten different views of him, but this is my story.

As I started reflecting on my life, the title of this book, *While Angels Were Watching*, was revealed to me, because their protection and guidance were evident throughout, and my father was one of them. He would never let anything go on in our lives that he was not aware of or a part of and he did not hesitate to give his advice when needed. I must admit that he did not interfere unless he was invited. Most of the time, we would gladly tell him everything because we sincerely believed that "daddy would fix it." Until his death, he did just that!

So, here are a few snippets of my life which will certainly show you that when you put God first, keep the faith, and give Him the praise and the glory, His angels will be watching over you as well. His goodness has been exemplified time after time, and I will keep on trusting and depending on Him because there is nothing better. This is what I learned from my father.

Every morning, when my father awoke and he was not out of town on a trip, he would have his own personal prayer service. He would thank God for his safe journey, for watching over his family while he was away, and for the blessings bestowed upon all of us. So, again, I had a living example.

Although he was not a Bible-carrying preacher type (he was the complete opposite), he'd steal away and get his praise on. He was never ashamed to tell anyone what he believed, because he could quote the Bible, Scriptures, and verses without hesitation. I guess that this could have been because he was the son of a "preacher" man.

I hope that you will find something in some of these pages that will help to encourage you, strengthen your faith, or at least make you smile. As I took my pen in hand, I had to stop periodically and ask God to guide me so that this book will be a blessing to someone and that I would also glorify Him by showing people just how wonderful He is. He doesn't just love me and my dad, He loves you, too. So, sit back and enjoy this trek through our lives, and as you do, I hope that you will be inspired. Blessings to you.

• • •

Where shall I begin? I guess that the best place to begin is at the beginning, so here goes. I am one of ten children born to my parents. I was fortunate enough to be number seven. It has always been said by some that the seventh child was considered to be the "special" child and by others to be the "weird" child. However, I never considered myself to be either. I was just the "middle" child. My brother, who was three years my senior, used to say that I was weird and that I deserved that title because I was never afraid of the dark, ghosts, or spirits, which frightened most young kids, especially my brother. Of course, I never paid much attention to what he or anyone else said, because I thought of it as pure nonsense.

As the middle child, I was the one sandwiched between the older siblings and the younger siblings. I was the child with a tremendous quest for knowledge and longed to see faraway places. I loved to read because it took me out of the peach orchards of Georgia and into a world of oceans, ships, airplanes, and unexplored territories, all of which I felt I had to see and experience. I never wanted to be like everyone else, who had no dreams beyond the Georgia state line, like most of my friends and family. I wanted to follow my dad's advice and explore the big world out there.

Living in "small-town America" limits you to the point that you can become so bogged down in nothing to where it is hard to see beyond where you are. This was evidenced by the amount of people who had no drive, no expectations, no motivation, and no dreams beyond our small town. I, again, was blessed to have my father, because as a long-distance truck driver, he came home with tales of his travels and fed my spirit to go beyond where I was.

Keep in mind that my father was the *head* of our family. What he said was the law, whether on the road or at home. He was the only driver cited for forty-plus years behind the wheel without a ticket or an accident. He was family man who raised his family with a firm hand and was highly respected by all who knew him and was beloved by his children. Everyone knew that if they bothered us, they would have to deal with him, and when it came to his children, he did not play! He was very protective and only wanted the very best for us. His favorite expression was, "If a man's word is no good, then he is no good." People who knew him knew that his word was his bond, and if you crossed him, you would pay. He gave respect and would accept nothing less from anyone else.

For example, if my father told you that on Thursday, he would meet you and pay you for work that you had agreed to do while he was away, you could count on the fact that on Thursday, he would be there to pay. If he told his kids not to act up at school, and that if they did, he would come there and get on them in front of the whole school, then you and all of the teachers could count on that, also. He said what he meant and meant what he said.

He had other Frank-isms. He would say, "It is easier to live with a decision that you make than one that someone else made for you," "Be careful who you hang out with and don't hang out with people that you can't take home with you," "Stand up for what you believe in, because everyone should believe in something," "Get as much education as you can, because people can take lot of things away from you, but they can never take your education away," and "Take pride in what you do, regardless of what it is."

There was an incident that stands out in my mind. When I was about eight years old, my father broke his rule and allowed me to spend the night with a cousin-friend. He had a rule that we should stay home, because everyone was poor, and going to someone else's house to eat, sleep, or use utilities was taking away from them when we had a home that was safe, clean, warm and had plenty of food. That day, when I asked, he said that I could go and spend the night with my cousin-friend. On Saturday morning, we got up, got dressed, and headed into town. While there, her parents shopped and gave us money for ice cream from the drugstore. Once we got our ice cream, we proceeded, as any eight year old would, to go to the area set up for kids by the window and took a seat.

What a big mistake! All hell broke loose, and the manager and customers started to yell and throw things at us. We were terrified, and did not know why they were chasing us, but we wanted to make sure that they did not catch us. We could not believe that grown men would act like that toward children. We knew that her parents were next door at the store, and we were running like crazy to get there!

Out on the street, I don't know if the wife of my father's boss was in the drugstore or not to witness the incident, but my father's boss' wife stopped me and asked if I was his daughter. She should have known, because I was summoned to her house often to entertain her daughter when she was bored. She asked me again and I said, "Yes, he is my father." At that time, I did not realize that in the South, everyone was expected to say, "Yes, ma'am," to white women. At her house, she rarely spoke to me, so I never said much of anything to her, and I did not realize that saying, "Yes," was an issue, and certainly did not know that it was an offense.

She grabbed me by my collar and proceeded to call my father at work and asked him to come downtown immediately. The last thing that I wanted was for my father to be notified that I was in trouble, especially when I did not know what I'd done wrong. This just happened to be one of those times when he was home and not working out of town. While we waited for my father, she kept asking me if I was his daughter, and I just kept saying, "Yes!" She finally informed me that she could not believe that I was being that disrespectful and wanted to know why I kept saying, "yes" to her like that, because "his children knew better." I responded that it was because my father had told us that that was the way to respond to adults. She became more outraged at this point. She could hardly wait for my father to arrive, and I dreaded that moment!

When my father arrived, she asked him if he had told his children to say "yes" to adults, and he responded, "Yes, ma'am." She asked why had he taught his children to respond in a correct manner. He looked her in the eye and said "I have said enough 'yes ma'ams' and 'yes sirs' for all of my children to last a lifetime and I felt that my kids should never have to say it again. I've said it to kids young enough to be my grandchildren." She wanted me to apologize, but he refused. He said, "No, ma'am, because she did exactly what I told her to do, so she does not have a reason to apologize. She did not disrespect you, she only did what I told her to do." She became even more outraged and told my father that she was getting him fired.

At this point, I started to cry and told him that I'd apologize, but he said to shut up and that he meant what he said. She stormed off. My father said, "If she wants to get me fired, then I can't stop her, but my children will do what I say to do." I did not have the heart to tell him about the grown men chasing us from the drugstore and down the street, throwing things at us.

It was a long time before we realized what we had done wrong! You see, those chairs were meant for "whites only" to sit in and eat ice cream, and we thought that they were for "children only!" Two Frank-isms apply here: "Stand up for what you believe in, because everyone should believe in something," and, "It is a poor man that does not rule over his own house."

Nevertheless, my father was not fired, but to this day, I never returned to that drugstore, nor did I mention the incident to my father, because I knew that he would have gone back to that drugstore and he probably would have been killed or killed someone else. I also learned a valuable lesson on that day: my father was a man of principles, and he practiced what he preached! He was an example that I am so proud to follow. He was honest, hardworking, kind, loving, dedicated to his family, and looked out for others in the community when they were in need. He sometimes fed the multitude! From him, I've learned to be strong, to believe in myself, to put God first, to rule my own house (if there was not a husband present), to know that I did not need a husband or a man to be whole or to be successful in life, and what respect looked like. His Frank-ism, "It is a poor man that does not rule his own house," served as a model for me as I established my own home. He said, "Without rules, a house is just another place to live and would never become a home, because anybody who enters can do and say whatever they want, and somebody has to be in charge." He strongly believed in family and often said that family will be with you when everyone else walks away. He taught us to be there for each other and taught us the Frank-ism, "Always put God first in all things, because God never walks away from us, we walk away from Him."

Long after my father died, I could still hear the echoes of his teachings, and I've often told my children, "You are the offspring of someone special; therefore, you are special." I gathered these teachings from his strength and his undying support. He pushed us because he wanted more for us than he ever had. He wanted us to have it all! For a man with a third grade education, he traveled all over the United States in his truck and could barely read and write more than his name, but could work math problems in his head just as fast as anyone could with a calculator. He was a giant man in a five-foot nine body who never weighed more than one hundred and fifty pounds soaking wet, but he was a giant of a man. He is the only man that could drive up to the school, and a quiet would fall over the whole building, because everyone knew that he would get anybody that got into trouble when he was called to the school and would get those who poked fun at the ones who got into trouble. His presence was felt even if he simply came to drop off lunch money or to check on the kids once he returned from a trip. He left very big shoes to fill.

As you can see, throughout this book, you will see me use the term "Frank-isms," which refers to all of his quotes that we would hear day after day, week after week, month after month and year after year. The "isms" were so ingrained in us that we did not realize just how much a part of our lives they had become. Some things become so automatic and so much a part of your life that you simply do not notice it happening. Then, one day, the things that you thought that you hated so much have become you. Regularly, I quote Frank-isms to make a point to my children.

Now that I've introduced you to my father, it will help you to better understand the things that took place in my life. I, along with my other siblings, went on to graduate from high school, and my father had prepared us to get out on our own. While in high school, civil rights workers like Julian Bond, Stokley Carmichael, and others came to our house when the heat got too much for them in Mississippi. If nothing else, they knew that nobody was coming after them at our house and that they would be safe, well fed, and comfortable.

After leaving home and being under the guidance of my father, for years, things would happen in my life, and I never really acknowledged them. I'd just say that it was strange, or that it was just my imagination, and let it go. Little did I know that God was trying to tell me something. All I had to do was listen and remember two of my father's Frank-isms: "When you graduate from high school, you must get out! You have no reason to stay around here. The world is a big place, and you need to see as much of it as you can," and "Don't settle for just anything, because you deserve the very best."

GOD'S AMAZING GRACE

Catherine M. Hill

I know not why the winds doth blow,
From whence they come or where they go;
But when I feel them on my face,
I know it is God's Amazing Grace.

I know not why the sea billows roll,
Why earthly cares take such a toll;
But when I gaze out into space,
Then I can see His Amazing Grace.

I know not why we live and die,
Why we laugh or why we cry;
I cannot save the human race,
But I'll always sing "His Amazing Grace."

Note: Once, as I was going through some changes in my life, my friend Ms. Catherine gave me this poem. I'll cherish her memory forever through her words.

2.

—————

A NEW CHAPTER IN MY LIFE
BEGINS...

I'll pick this story up after high school graduation. I left home after graduation and joined my brothers in Mississippi to work with the Civil Rights Movement there. The Civil Rights Movement was in a state of decline at the time, and I know that my parents were a bit apprehensive about three of their children being involved, but they just said that they would keep us in prayer. I was too excited and so proud, because I felt that my brothers had risked life and limb so that I could go to that drugstore and not be chased out by a bunch of angry adults: people who threatened an eight-year-old because she wanted to sit in the cool and eat her ice cream in a place designated for children. Yes, that eight-year-old was now an adult, and she was ready! Although it had been nine years since that incident had taken place, it stood out freshly in my mind as if it had happened yesterday

I was a field secretary in Mississippi, which meant that I received reports from the civil rights groups about activities taking place, where they happened, if anyone was hurt, and if so, how many, etc. Fortunately, or unfortunately, I became involved in the Civil Rights Movement at the time when it was coming to an end. As a field secretary, you were assigned a partner, and my partner was Tom, a white guy from Maryland whose father was a mayor. They assigned you to work with a more experienced person so that it would decrease the changes of you being discovered and killed.

We were in Jackson, Mississippi when we received a call at two o'clock in the morning. We knew that if the phone rang, it meant run for your life. The message was that the house was about to be bombed. This is when God intervened, because shortly before the phone rang, I got up and got dressed. Once the message was received, I quickly ran to Tom to make him aware of our dangerous situation. The caller said, "You are about to die." We left, running not stopping until we reached Lanier High School, where we hid until someone could find us. We had a check-in time, and if we did not check in, it meant that something was wrong, and a crew would be dispatched to find us, which is what happened.

They found us because Tom knew what to do to keep us safe. My older brother Frank was one of the people searching for us. He was terrified and told me that I had to leave. He did not want to be responsible for delivering a message to our parents that their daughter was dead. You see, the next day, when my friends Ben and Carol were registering voters, they were caught, and Ben was used for target practice. He was said to have been shot fifty-seven times, and he was only twenty-three years old. You never hear his name or read about him, but I will never forget him. This was my last day in the field. My brother was on the road making speeches and raising money and I had to go with him. That did not last very long, because everything was coming to a close.

I was about to take on a new chapter in my life. In the fall, I enrolled in college, far away from the movement, along with other women who were also there working in the movement in different capacities. We just wanted to be as far away as we could get, so when the opportunity opened up at a college in Texas, we jumped on it.

The Civil Rights Movement ended for me, and I enrolled in college. I felt displaced there, because while they were young and idealistic, I'd seen death, heard death, seen beatings, and seen numerous people displaced and begging for food and a place to stay. I'd seen unbelievable suffering, and in one year, I'd grown up beyond my eighteen years. I felt that my education had already taken place and that there was little that I could learn in college. I was no longer that naïve little Georgia girl. I was angry, and I kept pretty much to myself. I did not fit in, and I knew it before I even reached the campus.

I registered at the college in Texas along with the other five girls. It took some down-time for me to become a part of the campus life, but when I did, I loved it! Life was simple, my parents were far away in Georgia, and I was on my own! We were a giant family, and everybody looked out for each other. Although we were a different kind of family, the feeling was very similar to having blood relatives. You could go anywhere, and other students would recognize you as being from "the yard," which is what the campus was lovingly referred to. Once you were recognized, regardless of circumstances, you knew that someone was covering your back. After my recent experiences, I needed to feel this kind of protection around me, because I was no longer under the watchful eye of my father and family and learned quickly that life can be very cruel; there are no guarantees, and most people couldn't care less about your best interests. Therefore, the atmosphere on "the yard" was great. It was a refreshing change for me.

During my freshman year of college, I was thrilled, because for the first time, I was popular, which for me was something new in life. You see, at home, I had always lived in my sister's shadow. She was "queen this" and "queen that." She ran track, played basketball, and was a favorite of everyone. She was a living "Barbie Doll" with a petite frame, hair far below her waist, skin the color of caramel, and she was absolutely beautiful. When you have a sister that looks like that to compete with, although ten years older, a "plain Jane" just does not stand a chance. We easily get lost in the shuffle. So, that's what I did: I got lost in the shadows. No attention was given to me other than by my father and grandfather. I was reminded regularly that I "just didn't measure up to her" (not that I ever tried).

However, being in college was an awakening for

me. I was a queen! The guys thought that I was "fine," and I was sought after by some of the finest men on campus. The world had changed! Since I had four older brothers and a brother-in-law, I knew that guys go after you for many reasons, so I had to proceed with caution while I enjoyed my new-found fame.

No matter where I went, I never forgot that my dad was only a phone call away. I had to check in every Sunday before he left for church to let him know how things were going. The Frank-isms that applied here were: "It is easier to live with a decision that you make than one that someone else makes for you," and "Get as much education as you can, because people can take a lot of things away from you, but they cannot take your education."

During this time of recognition, I started to date for the first time! I had always been a tomboy who liked to keep her nails pretty and her hands nice. Other than that, the rest was up to God. At college, I met the captain of the tennis team. Not only did he look good, he also had a great sense of humor and was very popular. I could not believe that a senior student was chasing me—"that old 'Georgia girl,'" as he often referred to me as. Nobody understood his attraction to a freshman like me when he could have had his choice. I had to keep things in perspective because I could never forget that my dad's eighteen-wheeler could come to campus just as easily as it went anywhere else. I knew that distance meant nothing to my father when it came to his children. So, I would rather run the risk of being the "country girl" than to be known as one who knew no boundaries and weighed every opportunity accordingly.

Bob the tennis player was my first real boyfriend as well as the most popular. He would have been one that my father would have approved of, had I had the courage to take him home. He taught me about caring affection and self-respect, things that my father also instilled in me. He was my boyfriend and protector, and I felt that he truly cared about me. He was great! Cinderella only needed a ball! I had been forewarned that he would only use me, and once he did, he would forget my name. Fortunately for me, my daddy raised me well. I played it cautiously. After a long pursuit, I agreed to go out with him and left campus for a party. I was the only freshman there and got quite nervous about possibilities. I quickly realized that I was out of my league, but I played it as if I was a master. I kept in my mind that my father was only a phone call away, and I didn't want him to know that I was at a party that he never gave me permission to attend. I was trying to think of ways out if something happened, like how to get back to school, how to explain where I was, etc. I was a wreck.

He introduced me to all of his friends, and it was the first time he had bragged about me and referred to me as "his girl," which to me was the supreme compliment, especially since I had always been the "plain Jane." It felt good and I was having a great time. I was still silently contemplating what would happen at the end of the date. Meanwhile, he left for the little boy's room, and one of the guys asked me to dance, but I said, "No thanks." The guy got loud and started to tell me that I thought that I was too good for him. Bob heard the commotion as he was returning and asked him to apologize to me. The guy refused.

There I was in the city: I did not have a clue as to where I was, I did not have my parents' permission to be there, I was in a place that I should not have gone, none of my friends were there, I did not have a phone, and none of my friends had a car, even if I had called them. Then the fight started between Bob and the guy.

He said that nobody would talk to "his girl" that way. All I visualize was us going to jail, and there was no way that I could explain this to my father! I couldn't believe it! I just started to run. I thought that perhaps I'd find a policeman or somebody to give me a ride, because busses had stopped running. I got to the street, and a man driving a Hearst gave me a ride and a lecture about being out at night by myself. Only God could have sent him, because I later found out that I was in a very dangerous area and anything could have happened to me. My only concern was what my dad would have done to me had he found out!

• • •

I have many faults, but no regrets.

- Mother Teresa

I made it through my first year of college and had so much fun that I could not believe that college could be this good. Although I did not go to any more parties off campus, it was a good year. I returned home and received letters from Bob almost daily. I could hardly wait to get back to school so that I could see him. For me, once I returned to school, I knew that life would be good. I could once again make my own rules, manage my own money, pay my own bills, and to live life to the fullest. I made friends during this time that I still have today: true friends, because associates could not have lasted this long. Also, keep in mind that my father's rules still followed me everywhere I went, so I never smoked, drank, or did drugs, because I was confident that my father's reach was still long enough to strike. I dated (something that I could not do at home), stayed out as long as I wanted, never borrowed from anyone, and had lots of good clean fun. Always cognizant of my father and his teachings, I remembered the Frank-isms, "Raise your children up in the church. They won't understand it while they are young, but when they grow up, they will appreciate it," and "Keep God first and foremost in your life, and everything else will fall into place." Once again, he was right!

Just before my sophomore year began, I received a dreaded call from Bob. This call was just the beginning of a love tale gone bad! He informed me that his old girlfriend was now pregnant, and his parents insisted that he marry her. I was crushed! How could this happen to me? I told him that I understood and that I wished him the very best. He got married, and I did not see him again. So, my excitement about returning to school was now crushed, but I managed to make it through in spite of the bitter aftertaste.

During my second year, reality set in! I had to come to grips with the fact that having fun was not my primary reason for being in school and that it was hard work: lots of studying, labs, and homework. Although I kept my grades up, I did not utilize my time very well. I was only interested in doing enough to keep my father in Georgia and keep him happy so that he would leave me alone. If not, I'd be on the next plane home. Don't get me wrong; I never got into trouble, I was never out past curfew, I passed all my classes, and I held down a job. My worse infraction was to write notes to the dean giving me permission to go home for the holidays with friends and roommates.

I was always conscious of my father's watchful eye. I knew him well enough to know that his truck would definitely find my campus if I was ever reported to him. I loved being away from home and making my own life decisions, so I did not intend to jeopardize my freedom, not even for a good-looking guy. The Frank-isms, "Persevere—quitters don't win anything, not even the satisfaction of having tried," "Pay your bills on time, and if you don't have money, you can still get what you want because your credit will be good," and "Take care of yourself. Don't ever rely on some-one else to take care of you. Be independent," all ap-plied here.

It was in college that I first heard the term "drugs." I knew people who sold them, people who used them, and people who almost died from them, but I've never been tempted to try drugs. I knew that there was no way that I nor anyone else would be able to explain this to my father. If I died from taking them, nobody would have been able to explain for me. So, I played it safe and just left it alone. As I recuperated from my loss of Bob, I was befriended by the most popular guys on campus; I don't know what the attraction was, but I enjoyed the attention. The captain of the basketball team became my "cousin" since we had the same last name, and all of his teammates looked out for me. It was a good year.

During this year, I also met my roommate who be-came my "little sister." She was an only child and had always wanted a large family. It turned out that she adopted me instead. I was invited to her home for all of the holidays that I did not go to Georgia for, and her aunt (her mom had died when she was born) had a room for me there. I spent a lot of quality time in Hot Springs, Arkansas, and although I had to write my own pass to go, I never failed to tell my parents that I had been invited and about how my trip going, and they were happy for me. We are still family today.

This is also the time that Don, James, Heather, Elizabeth and I became close friends. We did everything that we could do and stayed out of trouble. I've always kept things in perspective and enjoyed life to the fullest. The most memorable time that we spent together was the time that the cheerleaders were on strike and we had a big basketball game. Everyone was getting restless in the gym because the cheerleaders did not show up, so we took it upon ourselves to lead the cheers throughout the game. We blew it away! We also shocked ourselves. We had a great time. We were heroes. People who knew us could not believe that we did it! What great fun! If I suggested it, most of the time, it went without question: we did it!

During my junior year, I met Tony. My friends,

Don, James, Heather, Elizabeth and I were avid sports fans. We did everything together. One was the most popular of the three, one was the football star, and Tony was the kind of shy one. He was everything that I was not! He reminded me of a "big kid," and he felt safe for me to date. He was fun, affectionate, and the guy that most girls meet in high school; since I did not date in high school, I could not have met him. He was my "high school sweetheart," only in college. He was perfect for me because he brought no drama and no demands. He was fun, affectionate, and gave me lots of love. Somehow, he could not believe that a girl like me would be attracted to him because there were so many other choices out there. However, I felt that he was what I needed at the time. I recall the Frank-isms that applied here: "Take pride in how you live and in how you look—you never know who's watching," and "Don't try to fix other people, just fix you."

As in most relationships, time brings about a change. Demands begin to enter the picture. I was determined not to lose sight of why I was in college. I was in my senior year, and I did not want to blow it. As time went on, we spent more and more time together, I was getting weak, and his demands were getting to be more than I could stand. I did not know how much longer I could stay strong! I knew that I would not be the exception! I'd heard many discussions in the dorm about how not to get pregnant, but those same girls were the ones who became pregnant, so I knew that they did not know what they were talking about. I decided to play it safe and continue to say no. I only had a few months to graduation, and I'd make my father proud. I'd be his first daughter to have graduated college.

Again, fate intervened. I wanted desperately to go home for Thanksgiving, but knowing that my father had little money and would normally let me come home for Christmas, he would in no way pay for two holidays that close together. You see, I was eager to go home, because I had to find out once and for all if I was really in love with Timothy. He was my high school crush, and since I could not date during high school, I could only talk to him during school and occasionally on the phone. After graduation, for a summer, we did date. I'd known him throughout high school, and we really became close until he joined the military and was shipped to Vietnam. After that, I only heard from him occasionally. He did ask me to marry him before he went to the military, but I could not do it. I had a world to explore and he seemed to have no interest in anything other than being one of those "limbs on a tree." I was shocked when he joined the military. I was already in Texas in school and had been to Mississippi. I was not ready to settle down in a small town and become one of the "limbs on another tree." I would have died slowly, because that was not my makeup. I had exploring in my blood (which my mother said that I had gotten from my father).

Timothy was coming home from the military for Thanksgiving and had called me to say that he'd love to see me. I was so anxious to see him because I felt that if I did not, it would probably be the last time that I'd ever see him since everybody that I knew that had gone to Vietnam did not return, and if they did, they were often mentally disturbed, physically injured, or completely out of it. In my heart, I believed that he would become one of them. I wanted more than anything to get home to see him, but God had another plan. My father said no, and even if I had gotten the money from one of my brothers, I still could not show up at home, because my father had already said no. I resigned myself to the fact that I'd never see him again, which was not the case at all. He made it back safely, but still had some serious issues that he was dealing with.

Finally, my Timothy story came to an end, as I later found out that he was about to marry. I guess that being so far away gave him plenty of time to find someone else or to fulfill his mother's wishes. I thought that I knew him, but obviously not, because he was marrying someone from home and not in the military. How wrong I was! Tony was looking better and better all the time. You see, God knows what we need, and sometimes it seems that it is not what we want, but in the long run, it is what we need. He always knows what is best for us. I've never felt a loss when it comes to Timothy.

You see, it took him to make me realize that I had a man who loved me, and I knew it! His actions spoke volumes to me, and he showed me in more ways than one. I'd said before that Tony was what I needed, and now I knew just how much. I'd dated him for two years. I'd watched him make the transformation from boy to man. We knew that we had a lot of work to do, but felt that the relationship was worth it. I knew that he loved me and had loved me for a long time. I was not ready for a man-woman relationship, but I also could not let him walk away knowing that he loved me.

So, I married him. Nobody understood my attraction to him because we were so different, but that did not matter to me. He had a good heart and a kind spirit, worked very hard, and was always striving to do better. I was not sophisticated enough to know or want anything better. School was about to end, I felt that I could keep my secret until after graduation.

He gave me a ring that he wore all the time, and he swore that one day he'd replace it with a diamond. Well, that day has yet to come, but I still have the ring. He always said that he wanted to give me the very best, and I believe that he tried while we were together. We had a plan that we would pool our money because we both worked, and we could put that money away so that we could have a good beginning together.

Things were really good; *better* than good. He was so loving and patient, and I learned a lot from him. I had so many questions, and he seemed to have all of the answers; for a person like me, who was so naïve, he seemed very smart when it came to the ways of the world. I don't know how smart he really was, but he was smart enough for me—after all, I knew nothing. He was a warm and passionate man and a very good teacher. He taught me the beauty of love, and what I learned, I learned well

3.

—

GOD WIPES AWAY THOSE TEARS

"If the person that you are with doesn't make you a better, stronger person, that person's the wrong person to have in your life."

Bishop T.D. Jakes

Unfortunately, Tony could not teach me all of life's lessons, and the "lessons" learned in the dorm from those experienced girls did for me what it had done for them. From the very first time, I knew that the seed had been planted. I'd never felt that way before, and I told Tony so. He said that it was the fact that I was inexperienced, but I knew that life had been planted inside of me. There was never any doubt in my mind. As time went on, I told him again and he just patted himself on the back and said, "Job well done."

As days went by, he started to believe that I was indeed with child. At first, he was overjoyed. He had said that he would be the best father in the world. We discussed names, what the baby may look like, etc. I knew that we would have a good life. He had told me that he was raised by his grandmother and spoke very highly of her. He spoke very little of either of his parents. I thought from his conversations that his dad was dead and that his mother had remarried and moved on. He said that he was the black sheep of the family and that he and his sister were not very close until they were well into adulthood. Because he had older siblings, his nephew was his brother, friend, and confidant. I was learning the family history. You see, he had never met my family and I had not met his. We had a secret relationship because my father would have killed us both! Unfortunately, I know that all of this bliss would be short-lived, as the semester was ending.

I thought we were making plans for the future, but he was making plans separate from "us," and one day, he proceeded to walk out of the door. He went to his truck, came back inside, and gave me a long hug and a kiss and said goodbye. I did not realize at the time that it would be the last time that I'd see him again for two years. I thought that something had happened to him, and I had his friends and the police looking for him only to find out that he had gone because he wanted to. His friend called when he found out that I thought that he was missing to tell me that he had moved to Boston. Devastation is not a good enough word for how I felt!

Unfortunately, life goes on. I had to pay for college because the semester was ending, and in order to take my finals, I had to clear the bill. It was then that I found out that not only had he left, but he had taken *all* of the money from our account two days before he left. I was shocked! He had planned this! How could he? I trusted him! He loved me! How could he do this to me? I was too hurt. I just didn't understand. So, I cried and I prayed. What was I to do? I remembered these Frankisms: "Always pray for guidance. God hears and answers prayers. When you pray with a sincere heart, He knows whether you are sincere or not, so don't play with God," and "A man takes care of his family."

Now, I needed money to clear my account at the college, rent, airfare home, and medical bills. I was hurt and broken. Nobody could make the pain go away. I felt that even God wouldn't listen because I was so trusting and so stupid. I had walked into a situation with my eyes wide open and I was now receiving the consequences of a bad decision. My son was the innocent victim here. I needed money and I did not have the heart to ask my father, so I called my brother and he sent me the money. I paid my account and took my finals. It was only through the grace of God that I passed! Now, I had more decisions to make. I had to leave school because everything was closing, and I could not face my father.

I decided to go to Chicago and be with my brother. They immediately knew that something was wrong when I got off of the plane in December, wearing a sleeveless dress and shoes with no stockings; the dress was soaked with tears and I couldn't even tell them why! My dress froze when I stepped off of the plane. My brother put his arms around me trying to warm me and told me that whatever it was, it could not be that bad and that I could count on him to do whatever he could to help me. That made me cry even more because I knew that he could not help me put my life back together and nobody could undo all that had happened to me in the past few weeks. My brother stopped at the store in the airport and bought me a coat, hat, boots, and gloves. Snow was everywhere, and I was sleeveless! I just wanted to die!

I was there for a week, and I could not talk, would not eat, and could not drink. All I could do was cry. Finally, after several days, my sister-in-law told my brother that I had to go home because something was drastically wrong, and she didn't know what to do for me. So, my brother put me on the plane home and called my other brother to pick me up, telling him that something was wrong and that I hadn't said a word since I got off of the plane. They were scared for me, more so because I showed up in Chicago in in a sleeveless dress and no coat in December. Something must be drastically wrong, and they felt that daddy could get to the bottom of this if no one else could.

It never occurred to me that wearing a sleeveless, wet dress was not a good idea in December in Chicago. In fact, I did not remember putting on the dress or getting on the plane. All I remember is the pain in my heart that would not go away. No amount of prayer seemed to make it better. I became ill and was getting sicker by the day. I knew that I was going to die, and I felt guilty because I really did not want to do it at my brother's house. I was so sick that the stewardess sat me next to a priest who prayed for me the whole trip back to Georgia, only I knew that the priest could not say a prayer for me that God would even listen to. He was wasting his time, and I could not tell him, so I continued to cry and said nothing. The priest tried to convince me that God was with me and that everything would be okay, but I never said a word to him. I just cried.

My other brother picked me up in Georgia and took me to his house, hoping to get me in a better frame of mind before taking me to face my daddy. I knew that the real drama would begin once I got to Georgia. I would now have to make decisions that I had been putting off for weeks. I would have to answer questions that I had no answers for. Sadly enough, I don't remember the trip to his house, I don't remember getting off the plane in Georgia, and I don't remember getting into bed at his house. I do remember telling him that I needed to lie down. Other than that, I continued to say nothing. He took one look at me and became really scared. We drove to his house in silence. He took his wife aside and told her the story. I like my sisters-in-law, and in any other situation, I would have shared everything with them, but I could not speak, not about this. I would surely die if I attempted to because my heart hurt so badly. They were both just puzzled as to what to do.

Needless to say, my temperature shot up, and they had to take me to the hospital, which I immediately refused. My brother called my cousin, who lived nearby, and she came over and took me anyway. I was too weak to protest at this point. The doctor gave me medication and wanted to keep me in the hospital, but I refused. The doctor said that I had double pneumonia and that I needed to be hospitalized immediately, and if I was not, I would surely die. My feelings were, *The sooner the better*. I flatly refused to cooperate.

I was in a quandary still because I did not want to die at my brother's house, nor did I want to die at my parents' house, but I was too weak to make any choices. What they did not know is that all I wanted was to die! I did not feel that I deserved to live because of my stupidity. I started to ask God for strength to go home to say my goodbyes to everyone without giving them any information. I would take my secret to my grave, my baby and me.

I don't know when I got home, but I do remember that my parents were talking, and they could not imagine why I was being so uncooperative. I was always the good girl who never gave anyone any trouble, so they were puzzled by my actions. By this time, my brother had called from Chicago and told them how I was so sad and cried all of the while that I was there and would not tell them why, that I did not eat the whole time nor did I drink anything, and that I had a very high temperature. They put this with my other brother's story to try and piece the puzzle together.

I did not say anything, and I don't remember much more. I was too weak by this time. I had not eaten in weeks. All I did was cry! They thought that I must be losing my mind. They didn't understand why I had given up on life. I didn't care what anyone thought; my pain was too great to care. They were also puzzled because they were not accustomed to seeing me cry.

By this time, my heart hurt so much that it felt as though it was going through my body and I felt life leaving my me. I succumbed to the idea and I had no fear at all. I just hugged my baby that nobody knew about but me, and told him how much I loved him and that I never meant for this to happen to us. I repeated to him how much I loved him, that I never meant to do this, and told him what his dad had said before he walked out: "No matter what happens, I hope that you know that we loved you and never wanted to do anything to hurt or harm you, and we hope that one day you will forgive us both." I went on to say, "The only thing good about this is that we will be going together, and I know that I could never have aborted you."

I would take my secret to my grave, because I could not hurt my father like this. He was so proud of my accomplishments, and it had turned into this. He would want answers, and I had none to give. So, I chose to say nothing. My heart hurt so much that I knew that life was leaving me. I succumbed to the idea and had no fear at all. I just hugged my baby and smiled knowing that soon God would take us together. I explained to Him how this was best because then the family would be spared the shame and guilt of my stupidity. I didn't commit suicide because I knew that we could not go to heaven, so I just gave up on life. There was nothing in the Bible about that. I assured Him that He was the best of both of us. I talked to Him until I was finally at peace with death.

I was smiling for the very first time in months. I was ready and waiting for death to make its final visit. My only concern was dying inside my parents' house, but I was too weak to go outside and lie down in the yard. They would have to understand that I did not have a choice. This way, my family would not be humiliated, and my son would not have to live with a bitter, inexperienced mother who did not or could not go back to school and finish her last semester, who did not have money for milk or diapers, a mother who had no place to go but heaven; the only good thing was that God would take us both.

I was ready. I'd made my peace with God and had asked for His forgiveness with a smile was on my face. It was time. As I laid there, feeling my life passing away, I heard my brother say to my mother, "She is dying and I don't know what to do. What could have happened to her that could have been so bad that she no longer wants to live?" I thought, If you only knew! But he did not; nobody did, and they never would. He did not realize how much better everyone would be when this was over.

However, what I did not know (or was too sick to remember) was that *I had an angel watching over me.* By the doctor's definition, I should have been dead by now. I was weak, did not eat, did not drink anything, and did not take any medication, but thanks to God, the double pneumonia and a broken heart was not enough to kill me.

As I was drawing my final breaths, a white light surrounded my bed and an angel appeared and said to me, "How selfish can you be? This is your last opportunity to get out of that bed! You are being selfish and only thinking about yourself! You don't know what God has in store for that child that He blessed you with, so stop feeling sorry for yourself and start to think about your child! Put yourself aside and look at the blessing that God has given to you. Get up now, this is your last opportunity!" She then said that I must wash myself seven times. I told her that I could hardly lift my head, so I didn't know if I could. She repeated herself: "Wash yourself seven times and you will be healed! You and your child will be fine!"

I felt so bad. I was so weak, too weak to pick my head up off of the pillow, but I struggled to get up. I prayed and asked God to forgive me for my selfishness as I struggled to get up. My brother heard me and came running into the room. He asked me what I was trying to do. I told him, remember that I had not spoken to anyone in many weeks, that I needed to get to the bathroom and I need to wash myself (I didn't know when I had last bathed or used the bathroom). He was the one saying to my mother earlier that day that I was dying and he didn't know why I wouldn't want to live, so he was trying to get me out of that bed. I said to him that I needed to do it now! When we got into the bathroom, I told him to run me lots of water into the tub, and he said that he couldn't take my clothes off and that he'd have to get mama or my sister. I tried to stress the urgency in it and he finally got the message that I needed to wash myself and I told him to put me in the tub with my clothes on. I knew that he thought that I was crazy, but he did as I asked.

As I laid in the warm water, I tried to raise my arms above my head and I could not! I kept trying, and finally I washed myself from head to toe seven times. As I raised my arms to let the water fall on my head and run down my body, I began to feel stronger. With each stroke it became easier. I was on the road to recovery. My ills, my sins, my hurt, my disappointment, and my sadness were all being washed away. Not only was He healing my body, He was also healing my soul! My shame was leaving and my hurt was becoming less painful, but above all, my will to live had returned.

As I laid in that tub, I could not ask God to forgive me enough times. I wanted forgiveness for my selfishness: for making myself the priority and not my son, for weeks and weeks of self-pity, and for not appreciating the blessing that He had given to me, that precious gift of life which was my son. I said to Him, "You are correct, because I don't know what You have in store for him, but by giving me this second chance, I'll find out. Thank You, Lord, for saving us." As the water ran down, I could feel my body as it healed itself, and I continued to bask in what I called my "miracle water." I was carried into that bathroom and could barely hold my head up, but with each rinsing of my body, I was being healed! I was carried into that bathroom a broken, lost soul, but I walked out of that bathroom with God's grace and mercy, requiring little assistance from anyone. Everyone was amazed!

I knew that now was not the time to tell them what had happened, and if I had, they probably would not have believed me anyway, but I knew the truth. My brother asked me what I wanted to do, and I told him that I needed to sit in the sun. At this point, I was following divine guidance, and I wanted to get it right. He pulled up a large stuffed chair and sat it in front of the door. I sat down, and the sun shined down on me and it did the rest of my healing. My brother said that he'd changed my bed and wanted to know what else I needed, so I said that I was hungry. I didn't remember the last meal that I'd had. Food, which was usually my friend, had not been a priority. In fact, it never crossed my mind. Me being hungry caused so much excitement that he called to my mother and my sister (who was also there because she lived next door), and they all started to cook all of my favorite things. They knew then that I was going to be alright. I knew it too. I ate like a starving woman. I must have weighed eighty pounds by then, but I felt clean and I was revived! We were fine.

From that day on, I was not ill again. I never took any medication and had not had any prenatal care, but like the angel said, we were fine. Still, nobody knew that I was pregnant, and I dreaded the day that I would have to reveal the truth to them all. By now, my father had gone out of town on a trip and I knew that I'd have to tell my mother, which would not be a problem, and she could prepare my father when he came back before I spoke to him. In the meantime, I was not going to say anything. I had been silent all of this time; I could remain silent for a while longer.

I had lost so much weight that nobody would have

guessed that I was pregnant. Although I was very pregnant, I was still wearing my same clothes, and they were too big. Before, I wore a size seven-eight, and now they sagged. I didn't care, because I was now a woman on a mission, and that was to get my life back on track. I was making plans to take charge of my own life and to never give that power over to another human being.

Eventually, I had to return to Dallas to clean out my room. The school had been calling, so they knew that I'd been ill. I dreaded the thought of seeing Tony or anyone else. I just wanted to take care of my business there and get back home before someone noticed that I was pregnant. I could not even tell my closest friends. Fortunately, I did not see Tony, nor did I inquire about him. He was no longer on my priority list. I had a son to think about, a life to plan, and decisions to make, and none of these things included him. I had to figure out our life, and I knew that God would be with us every step of the way. That knowledge gave me a great deal of comfort. Whenever my faith became a little weak, God always showed up to remind me that He was there.

Finally the dreaded day came when I had to

break the news to my mother, and I did. I informed my mother that I was pregnant. It was one of the hardest things that I have ever had to do, and I knew that the worst was yet to come. My mother said, "Then we need to get you to a doctor, because you have been extremely ill and we need to make sure that the baby is okay." I assured her that the baby was just fine. I knew that she did not understand what I meant, and I did not want to argue with her. I just knew that I was married to a man who nobody had met; who had taken my money and left me alone and pregnant, and I did not have a clue as to where he was. So, I told my mother that I was pregnant, but to please not to ask me any questions because I had no answers. I just needed a place to stay until after my baby was born. She reminded me that I'd have to tell my father, which I already knew.

For the first time in my life, my father was disappointed in me. He did not put me out, but he did tell me that wherever I got the baby, he certainly hoped that I'd also get support, because he'd raised his children. I simply said that I'd never ask him for anything except a place to stay until after the baby came. It broke my heart that he would take that attitude, but I also understood that he was embarrassed and disappointed in me.

I could not change anything that had happened. I just had to live with it and focus on my baby; after all, I was all that he had. My mother tried to comfort me by explaining why my father had taken the attitude that he had. She went on to say that he had bragged about me to everybody because I was his first daughter to finish college and that I had always lived up to his expectations, but this time I had let him down in a major way.

All of this I already knew, but I listened to her. I knew what she was trying to do, and I appreciated her efforts. At that time, I felt that I had more important things to worry about. I had bills to pay, no money, and no possibility of employment because I would be having a child in a very short time. So, I started to talk to God, explaining to Him that He knew my situation, that it was not all of my making, and that I needed help. I needed help just long enough to get back on my feet, and I promised Him that I would do my very best to not disappoint Him or my father again and that I'd be the best parent that I could possibly be to the child that He had entrusted to me.

In the meantime, I still could not figure out what had gone wrong in my relationship with Tony, how this could have happened, how things changed so drastically; I just did not know. I just knew that I'd cried my last tears; I'd wallowed in many tears over it, and had even wished for death because of it! Now, I was filled with rage! As much as I had loved Tony before, I now hated him with just as much energy. If I had seen him, I would have killed him with my bare hands! Is that what love was to him? I knew then that I'd never love anyone again. I was through! If love, trust, honesty, respect, and commitment were not there, then that's not the kind of love or even the kind of relationship that I wanted ever again in my life! In fact, I did not want a relationship ever again!

Hurt had filled the place where love used to reside, and now hate had taken its place. I was as mean as could be and as cold as ice to all men. At that time in my life, there were no "good men" or "bad men," because they all fell into the same category: "no-good men." You see, I had been hurt more than any human being could have been hurt, and not only was I hurt, but I was abandoned and left stranded! How low can one get?

Up until now, I'd had no major problems, and the ones that I had had were usually taken care of by my father. I was at the point now where I had to stand alone. My father had turned his back on me, and the rest was up to me. I had a new resolve. I was down but not out, and now I looked forward to tomorrow. Yesterday had caused so much pain that I had no desire to look back! I concentrated on forgetting. I only wanted happy memories because I wanted a happy child. During this time, Tony started to call on a daily basis. I flatly refused to take any of his calls, so he started to talk to different family members and finally convinced them that we needed to be together and that he needed another chance. I didn't care about what he wanted or what he felt that he needed, and I was certainly was not interested in giving it to him. I just wanted to be left alone.

I gave birth to a healthy baby boy. I decided to give him the last name "Smith" after that of my father, whose name he was worthy of wearing. At the hospital, they asked me who I wanted them to put down as his father, and I stated that he did not have one; that I was like Mary, and I'd had an immaculate birth. The nurse stated as she started to walk away, "She just doesn't know whose it is." I called to her and said, "If you put 'unknown' on there or that I do not know, I'll sue the hospital." Thus, it was left blank for years. I knew that his father's name was not worthy of being worn by my blessing that God had given me. I was alone, I gave birth alone, and I'd raise him alone. However, I was not afraid of that possibility, because I knew that God had something special for him to do.

My son was an exceptional baby. He could make sentences by the age of seven months and was completely potty trained by then. I'd take him places and he'd start talking. He never talked baby-talk and he never crawled; people would look at him in amazement. They often asked why he did not crawl or walk. I'd simply say, "He is not ready yet," which proved to be the case, because on his first birthday, I took him to my parents' house so that they could keep him while I returned to school to finish my degree. While we were sitting there laugh and talking, he said "Look at me, look at me," and walked across the floor. He's been walking ever since.

This poem tells my story for the first half of my life. I think that it tells it all:

All I Did Was Cry

Wyvonnia Smith-Gorden

All I did was cry
As I looked over at the place where he laid
All of the memories came back and
In my head the memories played.
All I did was cry.

I couldn't stop the pain or the memories of
The fights, the misery, the pain, and the scars;
Of a time that was wasted and memories lost.
The more I thought of this, the more the tears flowed.
All I did was cry.

The memories washed over me again and again
For the love that was filled with so many holes
That rocked my body and devoured my soul.
The years of regret,
Looking for something that I haven't found yet,
The tears of years so long-gone,
And all I have left is emptiness, heartache, and the remnants of a song.
All I did was cry.

Where did love go? I had to look
At the places and emotions that it really took.
How could I let pain take over this space
As the tears came down from deep, deep within?
I cried because I'd had a lover, but never a friend!
All I did was cry.

I had to go deep down to the corners of disbelief,
Deep down to the wounds that could never seal,
Because there are no bandages in places where only God
can heal!
Deep down to the caverns of what should have been
To the abyss, where I thought that it would end!
All I did was cry.

As the tears came streaming down
My clothes were wet.
Unfortunately, they could not cover all of my regret!
How could I give so much importance to someone
Who had a place as if he held me hostage with a gun,
When in my heart I knew, but somehow forgot
That only God should have been there, and I'd left Him
out?
All I did was cry.

I lived in a cocoon built of innocence and joy

I was like a kid who had gotten a brand-new toy.
Wide-eyed innocence is what I call it now,
But "welcome to the real world"
Is what it showed me somehow!
All I did was cry.

The scripture says that all men come short of the glory of
God.
I felt that I'd been handed the shortest stick of them all
As I sat and reflected on what caused it all.
Some answers I will never have
But "Fix me, Lord," is all I could declare.
All I did was cry.

As the tears came, I looked to my friend.
He welcomed me with outstretched hands.
He said, "You have my shoulder to lean on,
I am your strength in times of weakness,
I am your bright and shining star,
I am wherever you are."
All I did was cry.

This gave me the strength to let go
Of all of the hurt and all of the pain
That had clogged my body and blocked my brain.
The healing had started, and I could now mask my pain.
The tears had dried up, just like the rain.

I could clearly see now what had once been lost,
I'm just thankful that it did not come at a higher cost.
My soul was intact, my spirit was good,
I felt like someone who'd moved into a new neighborhood.

I could see the sun,
I could smell the rain.
All darkness had departed and cleared up my brain.
I was singing and praying, where before there was no
song,
I was no longer living in what had gone wrong.

I now realize just how thankful I am
That God gave me another day,
A second change and a lot of grace.
I could be a better parent, a better wife,
A better friend, a better child, a better teacher, a better
servant!
I could provide a better life!

I'd cried away all of the regret, the pain, and the shame.
The tears had dried up and I was back on track again.
I thank God for never giving up on me,
For helping me to become more of what He wanted me to
be,
For not losing sight of whose I was,
For not succumbing to what had been done,

But for remembering whose I was,
And for reminding me that victory could be won.

No more tears for me.
I can declare my joy out loud,
Because when I start to feel down,
I just reach up toward the clouds.

"No more crying for me,"
I can truly declare.
I found joy because I know that God is always there!

4.

A NEW CHAPTER BEGINS

When you first start out in life, you are a young-ster who is dependent upon your parents, so the first part of your life is scripted by someone other than you.

As we live and grow, life begins to shape and develop us into the people that we are. The pen goes from their hand into our hand and we get to write the final chapters of our lives.

Ultimately, how life turns out is up to us. So, write your script with care, keep God foremost, and remember what the Bible says in Psalm 1:1 (NKJV): "Blessed is the man Who walks not in the counsel of the ungodly, Nor stands in the path of sinners, Nor sits in the seat of the scornful."

Write your ending with care and doused with lots

of love, thankfulness, charity, and love for family, and never leave God out of whatever you do. Always remember to love, never forget to thank God and others, and always keep the faith.

● ● ●

After my first son was born, I moved to Washington, D.C., found a job there, worked, and enjoyed my son. He was an incredible child. Once I decided that I had saved enough, I contacted the school and decided that I was ready to face my past and get back to the rest of my life. My son stayed with my parents for nine months. Prior to arriving in Dallas, Tony had called so many times that my family just wanted me to give him another chance. I called him, we talked, and he was convincing. He really wanted his family back. I was reluctant to meet up with him, but agreed. He said that he had a place and that I could stay with him when I arrived in Dallas. He agreed to pick me up at the airport, which he did, and we had a long, long talk.

I was beginning to feel excited and hopeful that this might work after all. I still had reservations, so I proceed with caution. Little did I know that when I arrived at his place, there were female belongings there, which he claimed belonged to his roommate's girlfriend, who he said used the whole house as hers. His roommate showed up while we were having this conversation and asked who I was, where Emma was, and when she was expected back. I asked him, "Isn't she your girlfriend?" He said, "No, she lives with Tony, and she was supposed to have gone out of town for something," and that he was trying to find out when she would be back.

Tony then told me this long story about how he and Emma worked together and how she ended up with no place to stay, so he let her stay with him, saying that she'd only been there a couple of days before I arrived and that he thought that she would have been long-gone before I got there. I only laughed and started to look for a place to live.

I couldn't hurt anymore, and there was nothing that he could do to disappoint, hurt, or ruin my life again. I just thanked God for showing me his true self before I wasted any more time on him. He simply wasn't worth it. I was a woman on a mission, and the only person that I was going to be concerned about was my son. I had to make a life for him. He deserved much more than the kind of drama that his dad brought into our lives. All he could do was give us money, but he never gave a dime, and I never asked. I was Frank's daughter. He taught us to take care of ourselves and that God would do the rest. He was absolutely right!

Fortunately for me, I ran into my old college roommate and I told her that I was looking for a place to stay. She invited me to live with her. She forgot to tell me that we would be sharing a room and not an apartment with three other roommates. At this time, I had no choice because I had no place to go. I knew that this, too, would be temporary. God intervened again on my behalf.

ANOTHER JOURNEY BEGINS

But my God shall supply all your need according to his riches in glory by Christ Jesus.

Philippians 4:19 (KJV)

After two weeks of searching for a job and a place to live, I ran into my old boss. I told her what I was doing and gave her my whole story. She sympathized and offered me a place to stay in her home and my old job back. Isn't God good? She allowed me to stay with her, let me eat her food, took me back and forth to work, and never asked me for a dime. She told me to save my money to pay the school and to send money home for my son, which I did! To this day, I am grateful to them because I could never repay them.

Soon after, I finally graduated from college. I did it for us and for my father. He was not as proud because of my extra baggage, but he saw that I was true to my word that I never asked him for anything other than shelter. I paid my own way and for that of my son. God's promises are true! When I got my apartment, my old boss signed for me and also for my phone. All she asked was that I did not disappoint her, and I never did. I went home to pick up my son because I now had a degree, a job, and a place to stay. Life was looking up. I enrolled my son in Mt. Tabor Child Care and he was the youngest child there. He was a very good student; he loved school, and the teachers loved him.

To my misfortune, however, Tony and Emma moved across the walk from us. We were that close, yet worlds apart. We were strangers. I'd never met Emma before, and I wanted to keep it that way. I did not bother them and I did not want them to bother me. When

Tony would see a guy come to my house, he would use our son as an excuse for coming over so that he could imply that we had something going on. He did not realize that that fire had been doused forever. The fool that he knew—the girl that he knew—was now a woman, and I had no use for boys in my life other than the one that I had given birth to. I am sure that he thought that I'd be a fool forever, but there isn't that much love in the world. He eventually found out!

For twenty years, he asked me to take him back. For twenty years, I said, "No!" The hurt became real again when I thought of him; I was so much better off leaving hurt where it was buried, and I did not want to dig it up and start over again. I'd had enough. What I did do though, which shows a tremendous amount of growth on my part, was forgive him! I called him up one day and told him so. He was mystified. Of course I did not do it for him. I did it for me. I could no longer hang on to the pain, and the only way for me to let go was for me to forgive him so that I could move on with my life. It was not about him; it was about my survival and my happiness. You see, God was using me again.

During the years, I know that it had to have been

God who watched over us, because there was a time that I just stopped going to church in spite of my father's teachings. I said to myself (or I justified it by saying), "It's too much trouble without a car," so I simply eliminated it. Finally, the day came when God got my attention! I went through six days and I could not sleep. I was so restless that I just could not understand why. On the seventh day, I found out why. The seventh day was Sunday, and I awoke early in the morning, tired from another sleepless night, when something spoke to me and said, "Get up, get dressed, and go to church." I immediately got up, put on my pink two-piece and some heels, and walked to church. I thought that I knew what was best, but I again was reminded that God always knows what's best!

I'd sent my son home to stay with my family for the summer. I had plans to enjoy my carefree days, but for some reason, I could not. I felt compelled to get out of my house and go to church, and soon I was on my way, walking toward Mt. Tabor Baptist Church. I liked Rev. Carter, but he hadn't been on my mind in a long while. As I sat there in the church, I was all into the service. The young adults were singing, and services were good. I was glad that I'd gotten out of bed because I was feeling at home. When Rev. Carter got up, I was already feeling good, and as he got into his message, all of a sudden a haze came over the church. I rubbed my eyes and the haze would not go away. In the middle of the haze, I saw my son reaching out to me, saying, "Mommy, help me."

I jumped up and ran out of the church. The ushers were following me because they thought that the spirit had touched me and they wanted to make sure that I was okay. What they did not know was that I was touched, but they couldn't help me. I needed to get home as quickly as I could, and I ran all the way in heels. As I walked through the door, the phone was ringing and it was my father. He was crying and he said to me "I did all that I could for him, you have to come home!" I asked what had happened to my baby. He just said that I had to come

home right away. I asked again, *What happened to my baby?*" He said, "He's dead, but I did all that I could for him. You have to come home!" I said to him, "He is not dead! God would not do this to me! Don't you let *anybody* bury my child, I'll be there as quickly as I can!"

I thought that I had a covenant with God. He'd given me this child, and there was no way that He was taking him away from me so soon! I was the best mother that I could be! I was angry with God. What had I done that warranted this? My child wasn't dead! He couldn't be! I don't care what the doctors had said, *he was not dead!* As I packed, I started to talk to God, and I said to Him, "If you want to punish me, please do it some other way! You can't take my child!" I had to get home. I kept telling myself, "My child is not dead! We have weathered too many storms together, so this cannot be!" I started talking to God again, "God, I am back in church, I'm giving You the praise and the glory, so *please* don't take my baby! I'll raise him in the church just as my father did me, I'll be a better parent, I'll do whatever, *but please don't take my baby!* I am leaning and depending on You, and only You can fix this." I was crying and praying. I kept saying, "He's *not* dead! I have to get home."

In the meantime, like me, when my brother arrived at the hospital, he was told that my baby was dead. He insisted on seeing him anyway. He said that when he walked into the room my son called him by name! He ran out screaming for the doctor or a nurse. He wanted them to hear him and to see that he was not dead. They came but they told him that he must be crazy because it was *impossible* for him to say anything because he was dead when he arrived at the hospital! My brother insisted that he had spoken to him and he wanted them to check him again. They finally put a mirror up to his nose and saw a faint breath! He was alive! He was in a coma, but alive. I did not know this yet.

I was a nervous wreck. I couldn't get a plane, train, or a bus, but I had to get home. I called my friend Sherry and told her what had happened and that I needed her to drive with me to Georgia. She reminded me that I'd just started driving, but I informed her that I was going home with her or without her. I had just gotten my first car, a Toyota, and barely knew how to drive, but that did not deter me at all. I could not get any other mode of transportation, I'd never read a map, had barely driven across Dallas, but I was going home. I knew that we would make it.

She came over and we left for Georgia. We must have gotten home in a record amount of time, because my father was completely surprised. I don't remember the trip. I don't think that we spoke to each other the whole way, we just drove and prayed. I was thankful to God that I have a friend like Sherry who dropped whatever she was doing to go with me. Only a real friend—especially one as popular with the guys as Sherry—would just take off in the spur of the moment. All I had to tell her was that my son was in ICU and I needed to get home. I reminded God that He'd given me that child, and when He did, I was told that He had something special for him to do. If God took him, he could not do it. My son had to live.

When I arrived at the hospital, my son was in a coma, so I was told. They told me the story about my brother, Matt, arriving at the hospital and being told that he was dead but insisting on seeing the body, and when he walked in, my son had called him by name. Everybody had said that he was crazy, but they examined him again and found him to be in a coma, but alive. When I walked into his room and touched his hand, he opened his eyes and said, "Hi, Mommy. What are you doing here?" These were best words that I could have heard. The nurse ran out screaming for a doctor because they couldn't believe that he was now talking. Another nurse came in to see for herself and asked him what he wanted, and he said, "Some ice cream." She laughed and said, "I'll get you whatever you want."

My mother told me that he had been outside playing and had come inside and asked for a glass of water. They asked him what was wrong as he dropped the glass of water and collapsed. To this day, they never found out what was wrong with him. He was seen by several specialists and was observed for weeks afterwards, but they never found out anything that could have caused it to happen. They never had a clue. I felt blessed, because he had been given back to me again. I truly do believe that God has something special in store for him, and one day, we will all see what that is. He's a wonderful spiritual individual, and he knows how good God has been to us and especially to him.

My son remained in the hospital for two months under observation of some of the best specialists around, but they never found cause for his condition. After many conversations with these doctors, I concluded that God had taken control, that there was nothing more for them to do, and that we were going home because their services were no longer needed.

That episode in his life confirmed that God did indeed have something special in store for him. I did not know what or when, but I was confident that one day we would all be able to see exactly what God had in store. All I knew was that God had spared his life again, and I was just along for the ride. As long as God is in it, I am good with it.

When my son was three years old, the doctors informed me that he had an incurable eye disease and that by the age of thirteen, he would be completely blind. He was to have regular eye exams, and as he became older, his glasses would become thicker and thicker. I never accepted this because I knew that God had given this kid a charge, and he could not fulfill it if he could not see (or at least that's what I thought). The specialist that my son was seeing informed me that the deterioration in his eyes was occurring much faster than he had initially thought and that his vision would be totally gone by the age of thirteen. I began to pray, because I did not believe that this specialist was the final answer. Only God knew what the outcome would be, and I put it in His hands. The doctor had told me to start preparing to deal with a blind child.

I began to question whether or not the plan that God had for him was as a blind person, and if not, that He would let me know what I was to do. He would direct me to someone who would be able to correct this problem for my child. As usual, God answered! One day, I picked up a newspaper that I had never seen before and there was an ad from a new eye doctor who had just set up shop in Duncanville. I can't explain why I had a paper that I'd never seen before other than that it had to have been in God's divine plan; other than that, there was absolutely no reason. I called the doctor, scheduled an appointment, and told him the story of my son's life with other doctors and what the specialist had just told us about him being blind by thirteen.

He was fascinated by what I had to say and scheduled an appointment to test my son's eyes. After he gave him a thorough examination, he said that so much deterioration had occurred because nobody took precautions to slow it down! He went on to say that he did not have any magic, but he could assure me that if I did as he said, my son would not lose his sight. He added that at this point, he would need special glasses and special contacts because they would have to work together to slow down the deterioration, and that my insurance would not pay for any of this. However, he said that if we needed to do one eye at a time, then we could do that.

He explained that the minimum cost for one eye would be $450 for the contacts and equally as much for the glasses, and that these cost did not include the examination, medication, or the treatments. He did not understand that cost was insignificant; my son's sight was so much more important, and I'd do whatever it took. God opened the door, and there was no way that I was going to let it close! So, cost never mattered to me, because if that was what he needed, then that is what he would get; I just didn't know how, but I knew that he would! That's what faith is.

As we left the doctor's office, I did not have a clue as to how I would pay for this! I knew that I could not count on Tony for anything. I also knew that I'd do whatever it took. I reminded myself that ministers said all the time, "God said, 'If you take one step, I'll take two,'" and I was going to figure out how to make my first step. I had more assurance than I had ever had, and I was not going to miss out on this opportunity. God had opened the door, and I was walking through it.

I ordered the glasses and the contacts and did not have a clue as to where the money was coming from. This was more money than I made in a month and I only got paid once a month, but I knew that I was going to have what I needed when I needed it. I just had to convince them to go on and do what they had to do, order what they needed to order, and to believe that I would pay them. They did. Now, I had to get the money, but from where? The day before the glasses and the contacts were to arrive, I received my first credit card in the mail, and my credit limit was one hundred dollars more than what I owed the doctors and the opticians! See God Work!

Behold, I stand at the door, and knock: if any man hear my voice, and open the door, I will come in to him, and will sup with him, and he with me.

Revelation 3:20 (KJV)

When they tried my son's glasses on, he smiled widely and said, "Mommy, I can see! I did not realize how much I was not seeing! I can see!" Then, they trained an eleven-year-old how to put in and take out his contacts, how to clean them, how to store them, etc. This was the time when contacts were just coming in to use. The words, "Mommy, I can see!" kept reverberating in my mind and the tears flowed! He could see! I knew that God would not let me down! He could see!

When my son was seven, I was a student working on my master's degree and I had a fulltime job. Life was good. I met my second husband. It was an okay relationship, but I once again listened to man instead of listening to God. Dr. Johnson, known as a messenger from God, called me up and told me that I should marry this man. Had I not listened to a man, I would not have ended up in a marriage that was doomed from the very first day. He and I were never meant to be! It was just a time in life when I let my guard down and forgot who the master was. God had always spoken to me directly, and I should have waited to hear from Him then.

I found myself in a situation where I was working three jobs, maintaining a household, dealing with an abusive husband, and going to school. I had to ask, "What did I do to end up here in a situation like this?" I was naïve enough to believe that if you loved someone enough, everything else would take care of itself. What a fairytale that is! What I learned from that experience is that *you cannot fix a broken man*. Only God can do that, and he must want to be fixed. Then, and only then, can he be fixed!

What shall we then say to these things? If God be for us, who can be against us?

Romans 8:31 (KJV)

No matter how much you love him, no matter how much money you make, no matter what you have, no matter how good you look, no matter how much you pray, no matter how much support you offer, no matter how much counseling you get, no matter how much patience you have, no matter how much he hurts or disappoints you, it's all up to him to want to be fixed!

I never thought that I would reach the point with a man—one that I thought that I loved—where I'd rather die than spend another moment with him, but I reached that point! I sat up one night after taking the kids to my sister's for her to babysit and waited for him to come home. Normally, I wouldn't do this; I'd just pray that he'd stay wherever he was and that he would not come back. I knew that the kids and I would be so much better off and that we would certainly be much happier. Unfortunately, he saw it as his life's mission to make our lives miserable! He wanted us to be as unhappy as he was, and he spared nothing to try and make it that way. I started to hate the sight of him! I would sit at the lake and pray that when I got home, he would not be there and would never return, but he always came back. Sometimes, it would be a day, a few days, or a few weeks, but he always returned! All I wanted was peace! I simply could not take it anymore!

Getting back to my thoughts of my husband that evening, earlier that day, the kids had gotten a puppy. He got the puppy and he gave them instructions not to take the puppy out of the yard. Of course they wanted to show it off, so they took it for a walk. I was inside making dinner and thought that he was outside with them, but he had gone to the store or someplace. Upon his return home, the neighbor stopped him and told him that his son and my nephew had brought a dog over and it had attacked their poodle, so they would now have to take him to a vet and wanted him to pay. They had a big blow up over this, and the boys came home and left him there, arguing with the neighbors.

Nobody in the neighborhood ever challenged my husband! He took great pride in his athletic body and his karate skills and did not hesitate to demonstrate those skills at any time. So, this was going to be a major issue! Hell would have to be paid for this! I went to the neighbor's and told them to bring us the vet bill and that it would be paid. I just wanted him to shut up, but he still wanted to give them a beatdown! I heard the thunder after he came home because he was livid! Thus, the neighbors finally saw the true man that lived in the house across the street.

Why the kids did it, I don't know. They were six or seven years old, and I guess that's what kids do. My son knew better, but my nephew had never seen this side of my husband! They decided to do this, and I knew too well that the wrath would be much greater than any reward!

He was loud, and the kids were petrified, looking as though they would pass out at any time. His son was so scared that you could only see the whites of his eyes, and he was shaking like a leaf on a tree! After my nephew had been sent to his room, my husband was now dealing with his own child, and his rule was never to interfere. This time, however, I had to intervene, because I thought that his son was going to keel over and die at any moment. I went over and put my arms around him and tried to reassure him that it was going to be alright. Unfortunately, that was when the wrath turned on me!

I instructed my son to take both boys into the bedroom and to lock the door, and no matter what happened, not to open the door. On this day, I stood toe to toe with my husband, and all of the pent up rage was surfacing; I wanted him dead! How could he treat a child like that; his own child? How could he?

I was trying to explain to him that the kids were excited about the dog and that they never intended for the dog to get into a fight, but since it happened, they were glad to see the dog defend itself. To his son's misfortune, his dad did not see it that way. He was yelling, screaming and punching holes in the walls because he was so angry, and I thought that he was losing it! He had just taken things too far! At this point, I knew that this would never happen again in this household again; if so, it would be over my dead body! I was beyond angry, and I went into the kitchen and grabbed a knife. He was coming after me; I knew it, and I wanted to be prepared. When he was like this, he needed a punching bag, and I was not about to be one! He could break dishes, punch holes in the walls, yell and scream, but he was not going to get away with physically abusing us!

Normally, I'd just shut down and let him have his tirade, but I was fed up. When he saw that I was going to fight back and actually try and kill him, he stopped and looked at me long and hard, like he'd never seen me before. I was swinging that knife and he was ducking. All that time, I was praying that I did not kill him, because if I did, the kids would have nobody. I just wanted him out of my life.

After this, he finally got in his car and left. I packed the kids up, took them to my sister's, told them not to tell her about the incident, and said that I'd be back to pick them up tomorrow. They were okay with that. They were happy that they did not have to stay there with him.

I told my sister that if something happened to me that she should send my child home to my parents. I was preparing for battle, and I was planning to win! When I got home, I sat down and I waited for him to return. I sat in the dark, waiting, but he did not come. He did not come the next day, either, but the third day, he came back, and I cornered him with that same knife. I let him know that if he ever did what he did that day again, I'd kill him in his sleep! I also informed him that I was leaving, because I deserved a better life than the one that I had.

He did not expect me to still be angry. He was the intimidator in the family, and I would usually just let him have his tantrum and did what I could to ignore him. However, today was a different day, and he was caught completely off guard. While I had his undivided attention, I also reminded him that he had said before that if I ever left him, he would track me down and kill me and my entire family. I wanted him to know that I believed him; therefore, if I saw him first, I'd kill him on sight!

> *Who shall separate us from the love of Christ? shall tribulation, or distress, or persecution, or famine, or nakedness, or peril, or sword?*
>
> Romans 8:35 (KJV)

> *Nay, in all these things we are more than conquerors through him that loved us.*
>
> Romans 8:37 (KJV)

• • •

Now, I need to tell you how our problems first began. It was on our wedding day when I realized that I had a real problem on my hands. First, his sister showed up at the wedding with his six-year-old son that I knew nothing about and left him with us. He even went on our honeymoon with us. Second, he threatened me and said that I had better not have any objections to him being there and that he would "deal with" me if I had anything to say about the situation. Third, I learned of his terrible temper on my wedding day. He said that if I ever left him, he would kill me. Can you imagine how happy this marriage was? This should have been one of the happiest days of my life! I was deceived, betrayed, and lied to, and nothing about him was as it seemed. What a time to find this out! He told me, "You have to play the game to get what you want." He played it well!

I later learned that not only was everyone in his entire family afraid of him, but the people at his work were too. His temper was awful! He had been so nice, so charming, and so interesting when I first met him! I had no way of knowing that he had been severely abused as a child, that he had been bullied, that he had spent his life trying to find his father, and that he did not fit in anywhere. He was highly intelligent and could get the best jobs, but he could not keep them because of his temper. My choices in men had somehow gotten worse! Now, here I am at a point where I am brave enough to fight for my freedom. I learned some valuable lessons, and I thank God that I made it out, because for years, he tried to get me to "come home," but I knew that we never had a home! It was two years of absolute hell!

I do thank God for showing me the way out of this abusive situation. It was two years of pure hell! I never divorced him, because I was through dealing with men! You see, when I stood all that I could stand, I began to pray very hard to God. In fact, I begged God to show me a way out as I sat there in the dark that evening after he went too far. I also asked Him for the strength to survive once I left.

I had many obstacles working against me, one being that all of my money was gone! I had scrimped and saved for years prior to getting married because my son wanted to go to medical school. Although it would be years before he was ready, I knew that it would be very expensive, and even if after graduating high school he changed his mind, I'd still be prepared for whatever he wanted to pursue in life. So, I knew I would need to save every extra penny that I got for this purpose. Unfortunately, I was unaware of the fact that my husband had discovered this account, drained all ten thousand dollars out of it, and closed it out completely! Every dime was gone! He took it without my knowledge and without my consent. He had also taken my paycheck, which I'd just deposited into the bank.

At this point, while I was penniless, I was determined! I was free! He was trying to force me to stay with him, but nothing would force me to do that because I was done. It just made me more determined than ever! However, since I was still technically married to him, there was nothing that I could do to recover any of the money lost.

5.

ONLY GOD KNEW

After leaving my husband, the only saving grace for me at this point was the fact that I would have another paycheck in one month, but I knew that I would not stay with him another week! I was getting out of there. I had no plan of escape, so I kept praying. I started looking for an apartment, strictly on faith! I was confident that God heard my prayers, that He saw my needs, and that He would make a way for me. When I finally found an apartment that I felt would be remote enough for him not to think of and that I could afford, I really prayed.

A couple of days later, I was sitting on the edge of my bed, praying. I was sitting there, praying hard, telling God all about my situation, when my father appeared in a vision, standing in the doorway. My father was dead at this point; he had died in 1979, so his appearance meant that God knew I'd listen to what He had to say to me. Previously, my dad had become ill for the first time in his life, and after the brief illness, he passed away. Although he passed, his presence has always been felt in my life, and although it happened in 1979, it still feels like yesterday, because it was one of the saddest days of my life.

The visions of my father were the one beacon that made us all feel that he was still with us in our hearts. He always wanted to take care of us. It seemed like after my visions, something significant always happened. My father was God's vessel to me. He was sent to show me my way out and to give me encouragement that I needed to do what I had to do. My father said to me that day, "You are making the right decision for you your child." I said to him, "But I don't have any money! He took all of my money from the bank, all of it!"

Suddenly, there was a loud noise, and a book fell to the floor. In that book was the exact amount of money that I needed for my down payment and the first month's rent! This was the goodness of God. I rushed to start packing and never looked back! To this day, I have never looked back! I packed what I could put into my Toyota and began my new life.

I went to work the next day; upstairs in the building where I worked, there were attorneys, and I immediately filed for divorce. Unfortunately, my husband went to the same attorney, held him out of the window, and told him that he'd drop him if he had to come back, and that no divorce papers were to be filed! The attorney called me up and returned my money, saying that I needed to keep my crazy husband away from him! However, God never left me, nor did He forsake me. After a while, he finally left me alone, so I really didn't care at that point because I had peace in my house and happiness in my life. Again, God never left me, nor did He forsake me. I remembered the Frank-ism, "God never walks away from us, we walk away from Him."

After leaving my husband, I lost track of his son. I've made numerous attempts to find out where he is, but nobody seemed to know; if so, they were not telling me. One thing that I did learn about his family was that when you left one of them, you left the whole crew of them. They would have nothing to do with you. However, his son was a part of me. I would have kept him, but his mother and father refused (although, in my heart, I knew that they did not want him). I still look for him, even now, and I pray for him regularly.

As for my husband, he went on with his life. He became a well-known photographer after retiring from the phone company he worked at. I rarely saw him, and only occasionally got a call from him. About six years ago, he finally realized that I was not "coming home." We would still have occasional conversations, because he had gotten a lot of counseling and wanted me to know that he had changed. I was happy for him.

• • •

I cannot say that life was easy all of the time, because it was not! However, what I was doing for my child and for my sanity was well worth the sacrifices that I had to make in order to make it. I never lost sight of the fact that my child was entrusted to me by God for only a short while, and after that, he would become an adult and I would return him to God. During this time, I had to do my very best for him, and I've always taken that role very seriously. When I couldn't afford after school care, I worked the morning shift at school so that I could have free after-school care, and if I only had money for one meal, that one meal was for my child, because I have always believed that I have enough fat reserves to last much longer than he ever would. Knowing this, I could smile as I watched him eat.

God is always moving in my life. You see, at one time I was in between jobs and I was seriously worried about my rent payment. My job had shut down and I was searching everywhere trying to find another. Again, I began to pray because I could not see where anything jobwise was headed my way. I knew that eventually it would, but that had nothing to do with bills that needed to be paid now.

I had to face my landlord at the end of the month, and things did not look good. As I ran out of days, with only a matter of hours remaining to deal with my landlord, my doorbell rang at two o'clock in the morning. I knew that it had to be an emergency, because nobody came to my door at that time unless it was urgent. I ran to the door, opening it, and there stood my former coworker. We had worked together a few years before; he had borrowed money from me and had disappeared.

I later learned that my coworker's wife had cancer and that he had to take her out of state someplace, so that was where he disappeared to. Whether it was true or not, I knew that I had not seen him in years since he borrowed the money from me.

I asked what he was doing at my door and how he found me. He asked me, "Didn't you always live here?" I answered, "No," and said that I had been there less than a year. He couldn't explain how he found me, but this is what he had to say. He said that he was driving down the freeway in Dallas, and as he was driving, a voice kept saying to him that he needed to pay me and that he needed to do it that night! He said that he never forgot that I was a single parent and needed my money, but circumstances did not permit him to pay it before now. Since the voice would not go away, he started driving around looking for my apartment.

Keep in mind that there was no way that my co-worker should have found me, because I had moved twice since I saw him and had been in my apartment only a few months before he came to my door. He went on to say that he drove until he saw my car, which was not in an assigned parking spot because there were none in my complex, and that's how he found my apartment. That night, this was more convincing than anything that it was God who guided him to me because my car was not parked anywhere near my apartment, and since all of the units looked alike, he had to have had divine guidance to my door! He said that the only door that he came to in that whole apartment complex was mine! It had to have been God.

Needless to say, when my coworker left, I had my rent money, my car note, and money for my child's school and food! From that night to now, I've never seen or heard from that coworker again! All I could say was, "Thank You, Lord!"

After that, life was good; we were happy, and above all, I had peace of mind! My son was doing good in school and I was working and going to school. God blessed me with a good kid, because he has been to work, board meetings, committee meetings, school, etc., and he was just incredible. I couldn't afford to hire someone to keep him, so I trained him to be flexible and to be quiet when I told him to. He became the invisible part of me who went everywhere, so much so that people would ask, "Where is your baby?" if I did not have him with me. Another blessing!

During this time of peace and tranquility, one day, I was home mopping the floor when all of a sudden, once again, my father appeared to me in a vision that was as clear as day. He said that he had a message for my sister. I asked, "Which sister?" He told me which one and proceeded to give me the message for her. He said that it was very important that she got this message right away, so I asked him, "If this message is that important, why didn't you tell her yourself?" She would think that I was crazy if I called her to tell her that our daddy—who was deceased—had left a message for her. He said that if he appeared to her, she would be afraid and would not listen to what he had to say.

Being the obedient child, I called my sister and told her what had happened and that I had a message for her from "daddy." Of course, she started yelling, "You are crazy!" and I said to her, "Maybe, but this is what he said," and proceeded to tell her what he had told me. I told her that daddy had said that she would know what this message meant. Evidently, she knew, because she started to scream, threw down the phone, and ran away as soon as I told her. I don't know to this day what that message meant, but she certainly did!

A few weeks later, her roommate called me to say that she did not know what I had said to my sister, but she was certainly glad that I had called, because it made a major difference in what my sister was doing, and she had definitely needed to hear what I had to say. That affirmed to me that daddy was still watching over us, because that's the kind of father that he was. He protected his children, even as adults. I know that God uses him as a vessel to get his messages through, and I am glad that I was the chosen instrument that time. I did not know what was going on in my sister's life, but God did; He wanted it to stop, and He stopped it! I can only give Him the praise and the glory. To this day, my sister and I have never discussed this incident again.

● ● ●

I've had times in my life when I've needed money for food, rent, or school, and it would miraculously appear. That's why I put my faith in God, because I know that He will listen when others are too busy, will help when others turn their backs, or be a comforter when comforting is needed. Another good example of this is a time when my job had all of its assets frozen by the IRS; we were unable to get paid and did not know when we would get paid or if we would even be paid. We only knew that at some point, we would get our money, or so we hoped; "when" was the question. It had been weeks; I needed to get food and I needed to get it quickly, because we were down to the bare minimum.

One day, at about eight o'clock in the evening, there was a knock at the door and two friends were standing there. They had heard about the funds for my job being frozen by the IRS, and they thought that they would stop by and pay me the money that they owed me and would thank me for being so kind to them when they needed it. They paid me and gave me an extra hundred dollars, telling me that it was a gift. All I could say was, "Thank You, God," because they were right on time. All of our needs were met.

6.

———

FORGIVENESS

During the time that I was struggling with my son's possible blindness, I discovered that I was pregnant with my second child. I felt that God must have had a real good sense of humor because He knew what kind of mother I was the first time and what a struggle it was, and now I was about to do it again! I've heard of having a second time to "get it right," but that was one thing that I didn't feel that I needed to get more experience in. However, God had another plan. When I met the father, he claimed that he could not have children! Since I was still the Georgia bumpkin, I believed him. He was a man nineteen years my senior, was highly respected in the workplace, the church, and the community, was very intelligent, and was introduced to me by my best friend. I had no clue that he played the game of deceit, and he played it very, very well. Little did I know that he used this same kind of line on the mothers of his three other children. We were all taken by him, only not at the same time. His youngest was five years old when I met him, which I learned later.

However, I must admit that God blessed me with the best that this man had to offer, which was an absolutely adorable son; my wonderful second child. This child became the light of my life, and everyone who met him fell in love with him. He always had a smile and was as smart as a whip. He was a charmer from birth and captivated everyone who came in contact with him. However, he was my "sickly child." He was born with severe allergies, and they kept him in the hospital regularly. We spent so many days and nights in the emergency room that the nurses used to joke that they always knew when he was feeling better because "he'd always start to smile." He knew them all by name, even the security people. A Frank-ism applies here: "Always keep God first and foremost and everything else will fall into place."

Just to show you how he was, at age two, I gave him his medication to take to school because the school would not administer it unless I was there, and

I could not leave work to give him one pill. Each day, he was instructed to ask to be excused at a particular time and take his medication before the lunch bell. He would watch the clock and knew when it was time. We had done the drill many times, and he had it down pat. He was in the hallway taking his medication, as he did every day, when a new teacher noticed him taking medication by himself.

This day, taking *one pill* became a major issue. Nobody seemed to listen to the fact that he had been doing this most of the semester and was just fine. I couldn't just leave work to give him a pill. The new teacher felt that I was irresponsible for giving him the medication to take, but I felt that I was being responsible, because the consequences of him not taking it were far worse than if he did. He was responsible enough to do it by himself, or I would not have entrusted it to him. I'd never endanger my baby or any other child.

I explained that all he had to do after watching the clock (they did not know that he could tell time) was to ask to be excused, go to the water fountain, take his medication, return to the classroom, and wait for the lunch bell because it had to be taken thirty minutes prior to eating. It did not seem hard to me. He could not run and play like the other kids, and the medication made him feel better, so it did not seem complicated to us. After that incident, he had to report to the principal's office and take it in his presence, following the same drill. They were amazed that he knew exactly what to do. He simply said, "I know how to take my medicine, I've been doing it all of the time." Another blessing.

As a child, both of his grandparents were deceased. He'd hear his brother talking about his grandfather, who was also deceased by this time. Out of the blue, one day at the office, I received a call from my three-year-old, and he informed me that he had found someone called "Granddaddy" and that he wanted "Granddaddy" to meet me because he knew that I'd like him very much. I was more than curious, because I couldn't imagine who this man was and why he was trying to be my son's grandfather! I did not know if he was a pervert trying to get his kicks out of some little boy or what. Fortunately, I got all of the right answers, because I later found out that his name was Leroy and that he and his wife had been best friends with Grandmama (my mother) for thirty years.

It appeared that Granddaddy had never had children; he was seventy-seven years old and nobody had ever asked him to be their grandfather, so he was honored to do so. He said, "How could I say no?" Granddaddy lived in Portland, Oregon and we lived in Dallas, Texas so it would be a very long-distance relationship, but he was assured that he could call him at any time. They were like two peas in a pod and had so much fun together. It was a pleasure having him in our lives.

Unfortunately, their relationship was a brief one, because upon Granddaddy's return to Portland, he was diagnosed with cancer; it was serious because it had spread so much that by the time they found it, there was nothing that they could do for him. His only request was to spend some time with his grandson. Upon hearing his request, we boarded a plane for Portland. We had been forewarned that he was bedridden and that I needed to try and prepare his grandson for that. He was too weak too do anything because he refused to eat.

However, to everyone's surprise, once we landed and my son ran up those stairs yelling "Granddaddy, Granddaddy," he was given new life! I had tried to explain that Granddaddy was not going to be as much fun as he was in Dallas because he was very sick, just like he was when he was in the emergency room at the hospital. He said then, "I'll take care of him and help him feel better." When he entered his room, Granddaddy had him climb on his bed and talk to him. It was as though the longer he talked, the better Granddaddy felt. We could hear them laughing and talking all the way downstairs. I was praying that if he succumbed while we were there that my baby would be able to cope with it; that's how ill he was.

It seemed as though God made Granddaddy strong just for this occasion to spend with his grandson. This visit was about Granddaddy and his grandson, and we were just on the outside watching and enjoying the show. They did not want to be bothered by the rest of the world, and they seemed to want to make the most of each and every moment together. Granddaddy was revived by his grandson and was very happy to spend time with him.

The next morning, to everyone's surprise and shock, Granddaddy got up, got dressed, and came downstairs looking for his grandson. We were shocked beyond belief! He had not been eating, and he asked my son what he wanted for breakfast! Whatever my son wanted, he and Granddaddy ate! Since pancakes were my son's favorite, I made pancakes, eggs, and bacon. They sat and talked and ate for two hours.

After breakfast, Granddaddy wanted to walk to the park so that he could push his grandson in the swing and watch him slide. He also wanted to show his grandson off to his best friend, who lived near the park. The park was a few blocks from the house, and Granddaddy insisted on walking there with his grandson. His wife was livid because she knew that he could not survive a walk that far, but he insisted, and they took off.

We followed in the car so that we could pick them up at any time, but God is in the miracle business! Not only did Granddaddy walk to the park, push his grandson in the swing, and watch him slide on the sliding board (his wife cried as she watched in disbelief), but he also got to show his grandson off to his best friend and walked back home holding his grandson's hand. Everyone watched in amazement!

Upon their return to the house, I made their requested dinner and they both ate and ate. We just watched. This is how it was the whole time that they were together. We knew that this had to have been a miracle, because granddaddy could hardly lift his head off of the pillow prior to our arrival, and now he had eaten, walked to the park and back, pushed his grandson in the swings, and introduced his best friend to his grandson.

We were there for two weeks; the best two weeks of Granddaddy's life. As we packed to leave, I could see the tears in Granddaddy's face, and I knew in my heart that his grandson would never see him again. I felt so blessed for their time together. His wife said that when we left for the airport, he returned to bed, never got up or spoke again, and a few days later, he passed away. Leroy Robinson was a true blessing sent by God.

When my son was older, he always had a smile or a witty tale for you. He once said that he'd make more money than Eddie Murphy, the famous comedian, because he was so much funnier! People who saw him automatically assumed that he was very studious because he carried books with him all of the time. However, this was the same kid that received the "Top Student Award" and the "Class Clown Award" on the same day. That's the kind of kid he was. Unfortunately, his dad did not get to see either side. He chose to remain distant, and we gave him his space.

As my son became older, his dad used to call him

and promise to pick him up, but never showed. He would pack his little bag and wait and wait and wait. He didn't want to leave his spot on the front stoop because his dad was coming, and he rarely showed! However, God had another plan.

One day, God sent Jim into our lives. He had befriended Grandmama and was doing work for her, so that's how they'd met. Jim was absolutely fascinated by this little kid with the big vocabulary who carried on a conversation like and adult, but was only two years old. He did not realize that this kid had been talking since he was six months old. I guess that he always knew that he would have lots to say, so he just started early.

During one of his conversations with Jim, he had told him that his dad was calling him to come and pick him up, but that he would not show up. So, Jim took it upon himself to watch while he waited for his dad on the stoop. If his dad did not show, Jim would pretend to be driving by and he'd ask him to go for a ride with him (he had already cleared this with me before coming to my son's rescue). Once he knew that he hadn't been picked up, he'd drive by and scoop him up to run an errand with him. Soon, the subject of his dad picking him up became a mute tale, but Jim loved spending time with him and used to comment, "How could anyone stand this adorable kid up?"

Jim would spend the day taking him to the park or anywhere else just so that he would not be disappointed that his dad did not come. It reached the point that he and Jim would make plans because his dad stopped making those calls. This is how he became a prominent figure in our life. When there was an event at school, he'd ask Jim to come, and he always would. Whatever the occasion, it would be him and his "Big Jim." You see, Jim did not have much of a family life, so he remained in our lives until my son became a teenager. Isn't God good?

● ● ●

When my son was three or four years old, his dad married a woman with three children. Since he was now married to her, they decided to take me to court so that he would no longer have to pay child support! Can you imagine that? When I was served with the summons to appear in court, as ludicrous as I thought that it was, I knew that I had to file an answer. I called attorney after attorney, and the money that they wanted up front was impossible for me to obtain. So, I went down to the county to see if I could go about doing it myself.

They gave me such a runaround that I just threw up my hands in disgust. I was sitting there in the lobby, almost in tears, and I started to pray. I just closed my eyes; I was afraid that if I kept them open, I would be screaming in a public place. I looked up and said, "Lord, I've tried, but I cannot do this by myself. I need Your help. Every time I knock on a door, it closes in my face, and I have to be in court tomorrow morning, so I'm calling on You because only You can help me now."

Suddenly, a lady tapped me on the shoulder and asked me if I was okay. She asked if I needed help. I used this as an opportunity to vent. She said that her name was Faye, and she sat down beside me and listened intently to what I had to say. She never once interrupted me, and I told her everything. I just needed to let it all out, and she had a willing ear. I was trying not to cry because I was in a public building and I was known by most of the people there, so I did not want to become a public spectacle. She just listened, and I felt comfortable talking to her because she was a complete stranger, so I felt safe telling her my tale of woes. When I finished, she said that she had a friend and she'd bet that she would help me out. I explained that I did not have the large sum of money, nor could I get that kind of money. She just said again that she felt that her friend would be glad to help me out. She said, "Don't worry, I'll get her on the phone."

She called her friend Darlene and told her that she had someone who needed her help. She put me on the phone, and I told her everything, including the fact that I did not have any money. I did tell her that I was not trying to get anything for free, it was just that I did not make that kind of money, but I would be happy to agree to a payment plan of some kind. I told her that I was due in court the following morning at ten o'clock. Her response was, "That doesn't give us much time, and if we have to get it postponed, then we will." She asked the name of the judge and agreed to meet me at ten o'clock.

The next morning, I was there looking for her because I failed to ask her for her last name or what she looked like. I didn't know who I was looking for. I paced back and forth in front of the courtroom and I started to pray again, saying, "Lord, it looks as though it will be You and me, so I'll just follow Your lead. I'm beginning to think that Darlene decided that this was insignificant and that no money would be made, so she just didn't show up today. Although this is ridiculous, I still have to defend myself, not for me, but for my child. How could he do this to us?"

In the meantime, my son's dad, his new wife, many of their friends (only one of which I had seen before), and two attorneys were gathered there to go into the courtroom. I couldn't imagine why those other people were there, and I certainly didn't know who they were. So, again, I started to pray "Lord it's just You and me against all of these people, but I know that with You on my side, it doesn't matter how many others are against me. I am leaning and depending on You." Suddenly, I felt calm. I had never been in court before, but I was confident that God was with me! I relaxed and was ready for the fight, whatever it took, and I believed with my heart and soul that I would emerge victorious.

Suddenly, out of the blue, I saw this woman rushing toward me. She extended her hand and said that she was Darlene. She went on to say that she was sorry that she was late; she had to stop downstairs and file my papers before court started. She looked around and asked, "Who are all of these people?" I told her that I did not have a clue. She asked, "You don't know what they have to do with your case?" I said, "No. They shouldn't have anything to do with this case because I only know one of them, and she comes to church occasionally. I know that she's his wife's friend, but nothing more." I let her know that she was the friend that used to help his wife call me up and harass me over the phone, like school girls for some unknown reason. She said that it was still strange that all of them were there, but I could not explain it.

Once court started, she went up to the judge and whispered to her, and the judge cleared the courtroom, leaving my ex, his wife, and their two attorneys. She then made them dismiss one of the attorneys because they could only have one. The judge asked why this ridiculous case was in her court and his wife answered and said, "Now that he is married to me, he should no longer have to pay child support because I have three children and they need all of his money in their household." Up until that moment, I had thought that he was many things, but never stupid. Boy, was I wrong!

The judge asked, "What do her three children have to do with this case, does that exempt you from fatherhood of this child?" Before he could answer, she added, "Why doesn't she have the fathers of her three children up here instead of wasting the court's time on this nonsense! Don't you know—apparently you do not—that someone else's child does not negate your responsibility as a parent? Since you came here to deny your child, I am going to *double* your payments to him and also have you pay *all* attorney fees and *all* court costs." Not only did she double his payments, she made them retroactive from the time that he was six months old. I informed the judge that he had occasionally paid, and she asked him if he could prove it, and he said no. She said that from now on, he will, because it will be paid through the child support office. I gave Darlene a big hug and said, "Thank you." I also looked up and said, "Thank You, Lord. You knew what I needed, and You sent her right on time."

This is why I am telling this story. It is what happened next that proves that God was walking with me all the way. The next day, I went to the county to find Faye so that I could thank her and to give her a hug and to let her know how awesome her friend Darlene had been in court. When I got to her office, nobody was there. I started to inquire about her, and nobody knew what I was talking about. Nobody had even heard of her! I explained that I was at her desk the day before and pointed to it. That's when they told me that that particular desk had been vacant for several months and that nobody worked there. The person who worked there previously, named Faye, had died. They went on to tell me that I must have been in the wrong place. I knew that I was not! I then knew that God had sent His angel to help me!

Just to be sure, I called Darlene and asked her if she knew where Faye had gone. She did not know who I was talking about. I told her that Faye was the lady that had called her office and asked her to take my case. She said that she did not know her, so I asked why she took my case. She said that she took it because I was in a desperate situation and needed an attorney. She added that she did not normally handle cases like mine, but she just felt the need to help someone in a desperate situation. She had no idea who it was that called her! Isn't God good?

Thanks to that judgment, my son was able to tour Europe representing the U.S.A. as an Ambassador, travel to Germany, participate in school activities, play indoor and outdoor soccer, attend private schools (due to his medical condition), and graduate from a private university as a member of Phi Beta Kappa. God knows what we need, and the Word says in Philippians 4:19 that He will supply all of our needs according to His riches in glory. All we have to do is to do the right thing and just keep the faith!

Every job is a self-portrait of the person who did it, so autograph your work with pride and excellence.

Unknown

• • •

As time went on, God touched our lives in so many ways. My second son had been a very sickly child, as I stated before, so I was very protective of him. He was such a little charmer that everybody just loved him. His smile was contagious, and there were few exceptions.

In middle school, there was this guy who used to pick on him. I did not know what had happened, but I knew that my child loved school and never wanted to miss a day. This same child was now making excuses so that he could stay home. Since his excuses were not good ones, he went to school, but he would come home sad and declaring that he was not going back. Finally, I insisted that he tell me what his problem was. He then told me about a bully that had been picking on him. I asked him (jokingly, of course) if he wanted me to go to school and punch his lights out! He just laughed and said that he would take care of it himself. I asked if he had reported it to the teachers, and he said yes, but they said that he should stop whining and stop telling them. That did not make me very happy!

A few days went by and he was still sullen, so I became very concerned and had decided that I was going to the school the following day and solve his problem. I knew that my son did not bother anyone, and I wanted to find out who was bothering him. I also wanted to know why the teachers didn't put a stop to it. That day, he came home and he was back to normal. I asked him how he had solved his problem. He said that he had written the bully a letter and told him to leave him alone and that he did not want him picking on him again. He told him that if he wanted him to be his friend, then he should say so, and if not, he should just leave him alone!

Upon hearing this, I knew that my son was dead meat! Who had ever heard of a bully reading a letter, a ten-page letter? I knew that he was going to kill my baby! I went to work and told everybody that if the school called that I was to be notified right away. I told them the story and everyone laughed! They too expected a call from the school about my son, so we were all on guard, but fortunately for him, the bully left him alone! I called Jim and told him about the letter, and he said that he'd better stay close because he would have to go rescue him! We had a big laugh about it later, including the people at work!

• • •

Eventually, my son's asthma and allergies caused us to move from Dallas, Texas to Georgia. God blessed us with a good home, good schools, and a good job. When you don't know which way to go, just ask Him and He will guide your footsteps. Transition is difficult most of the time, but I had an advantage because I knew who I had on my side.

Although you know it, you can let the trials of the world make you weak. I had one such incident happen to me. I was on a job where I was the first and only minority ever hired, and I was led there by divine guidance. I'd asked God, and He said that was where He wanted me to be. In spite of the coldness, the pettiness, and the games played, I knew that it was God who was guiding my footsteps. I knew this; I was getting weak because I had forgotten that grownups can play childish games and sit around and plot against you in an effort to make you fail or look bad. I felt that I was in the devil's den.

I was naïve enough to believe that if you did your job, did it well, stayed out of other people's business, and stayed to yourself that you would not have to worry about other people. However, I had a bitter lesson to learn about jealousy. It is a means of destruction, and it was coming my way, fast. One day, I was so downtrodden by all of the recent events that I was on the brink of tears. It was because of someone else's mess, but I refused to let them see me cry or know that they had gotten under my skin. I quickly went into my office and closed the door so that I could regroup. Once that door closed behind me, I began to let the tears flow, took my Bible out of my desk drawer, and began to pray. I told God that I'd never done anything mean, cruel, or dishonest to anyone, and asked why they wouldn't just leave me alone! I did not care that they were not my friends, all I wanted was just to be left alone! I was tired, and I refused to let them break my spirit.

So, I prayed and I cried! My Bible fell open to Psalm 40:1-2 (KJV), which begins with these words: "I waited patiently for the Lord; and he inclined unto me, and heard my cry. He brought me up also out of an horrible pit, out of the miry clay, and sat my feet upon a rock, and established my goings." Tears of joy ran down my face, because I knew that He had not forsaken me! I looked up and said, "Thank You, Lord." Joy filled my soul, and I could hardly contain myself. I started to sing, "God specializes in things that seem impossible, and He can do what no other power, Holy Ghost power, can do." I sang until I forgot about all of the events of the past few days that had caused me to be so upset and forced me to end up shut up in my office. I was singing loud so I could hear voices outside my door. When I emerged from the office, I was still singing. Everyone looked at me with their mouths opened as if seeing me for the very first time. One of my co-workers even went so far as to say, "What does she have to sing about?" I just laughed to myself, because she wouldn't have understood. After praying and singing, my problems ceased to exist! Isn't God good?

One time, there was another incident that

caused me to become seriously depressed about the work that I was doing. Everything seemed to not work out the way that I had hoped. I was at the point where I was about to give up. I felt that I had given it my best, but it all seemed to just blow in the wind. One day in particular, there was a time when my bank account was screaming for more, and I just couldn't seem to get "more" anywhere. I was at my wits' end, so again, I prayed and said, "Lord, I've done everything that You have asked me to do and I've worked extremely hard to get this business going, but nothing seems to work. I just don't know what to do! I need help!" As I sat there, holding my head in my hands, a voice spoke to me and said, "I never told you that it would be easy, but I promise you that it will be worthwhile."

I had to laugh at myself, because it *hadn't* been easy! At least now I had the confirmation that I needed. I knew it would pay off if I remained persistent, and it did! As many times as I receive confirmation from Him, I still have my weak moments. I'm just thankful that He is God, because He understands and He forgives. Man will sit in judgment and still will not forgive, but God doesn't give up even when we do. We walk away, but God never does! All we have to do is lean and depend on Him and He will see us through! He never stops being good, merciful, and kind, nor does He stop wanting the very best for us.

• • •

I have been blessed in my lifetime to have a few good friends; friends who are there when you are "up" as well as when you are feeling down. I've got such a friend. I'll tell you about just two of the times that she proved to me that she was my friend. I am sure that she doesn't remember this, but I'll never forget.

Once, I was sick. I had been to the hospital and my own sister didn't have time for me, but my friend came to my house, cooked for my son, picked him up at school, and dropped him off. My friend had a job, husband, children and a life of her own, but she was there for me when I needed her most. I am sure that she doesn't remember this incident, but like I said, I will never forget it!

Another time, I'd just moved away from Texas, and my son was a student at Texas A&M. He called me and said that his scholarship money had not come in and that he was going to be put out of school if his bill was not paid in two days! Of course, I yelled at him for waiting until the last minute to call me, but nevertheless, I had to work it out. My bank accounts were still in Texas, and I did not have access to those banks in Georgia. I asked him if he had his bank card that I had given him, and he said that he had left it in his suitcase. His roommate had borrowed it and he was out of town. I thought, *Who could I trust to do this for me?* I called a few people to see if I could borrow the money, but their answers were, "No." If I had the money transferred, it would take a minimum of three days.

What was I to do? My son was not leaving A&M until he graduated! So, I called my friend and asked her if I could overnight my bank card to her so that she could wire the money to my son, as I was trying to avoid him being put out of school. She asked how much he needed and when. I gave her the information. She said "I'm off today and I'll take the money to him, so give me his number so that I can arrange to meet him and give it to him today! I'll replace my money when your card arrives and you don't have to waste money sending it overnight." I cried. I called my son and told him that my sister-friend was bringing him the money that day. He was to arrange to meet her and pick it up.

He was elated! They met and she gave him the money along with a few dollars for spending money! That's more than a friend, that's a sister! Isn't God good?

I have another friend that God blessed me with. I do believe that he was also meant to be my husband; it's definite that the other two were not! I made those choices, and there was no "God" in the choices I made! Anyway, I had missed work for several days because I had the flu and couldn't get my temperature down. The doctor wanted me to go to the hospital, but I had to take care of my child. I couldn't do that at the hospital, so I stayed home. Since we worked at the same place, just not in the same office, it was easy for my friend—whose name was Dell—to find out that I had not been there. He called my house, and I told him that I was sick. He wanted to come over, but I told him that I was not in the mood, nor was I presentable enough for company. I did not want to scare him because I looked rough! I'd had chills and fever for the past three days, and I would have been too embarrassed (if I hadn't felt so bad) for him to see me like I was.

When my doorbell rang, Dell was standing there, and I was too sick to be embarrassed! I just asked him to leave and headed for my bed. He asked if my temperature was gone, and I said it wasn't. He felt my head and said that I was burning up. He made me a tub of water and wanted me to sit in it (I now I realize that it could have been because I smelled). I followed his orders because I was too sick to argue. While I was in the tub, he changed my bed. When I was done bathing, he rubbed me down with Vicks and gave me Tylenol and orange juice. He went to the store and got juice and more soup. He called his secretary and told her to clear his calendar for the remainder of the day and the next day. He stayed with me, checked on me, and cared for me until he realized that my chills were not going away.

Dell took off his suit, put on my big robe, and wrapped me up in it with him to generate body heat so that I could sweat. Hours later, my temperature broke for the first time. He gave me soup, orange juice, and Tylenol, and went home to check on things. He later came back and helped my son with his homework. The next day, he took him to school, made him breakfast, and checked on things at his office. He came back and helped me get showered and gave me more medicine. He took excellent care of me and my son; I needed it and did not realize it. It never occurred to me that an attractive, popular guy like him would really be interested in whether or not I was sick. He was very much "in-demand," and I knew that for a fact! I took it as God wanting to show me that there was so much more to this man than how he looked, and I may never have known just how special he was had this not happened. Dell became a very special part of my life and did many other things to show me just how special he was.

I had met Dell in a data processing class during my sophomore year in college. He was a big-time running back on the football team, was a star on campus, and was a real "ladies' man." We became the best of friends when the instructor asked me to tutor him (she liked us both, so I believe that she really wanted to hook us up). In doing so, I discovered a wonderful man, a terrific guy, and my soulmate. I never knew that soulmates were real, but mine was!

Unfortunately, he did not believe it. However, Dell was the greatest love of my life and the best male friend that I've ever had. He was warm, giving, easy to talk to, respected me, gave me space when I needed it, supported me in my endeavors, and loved me in spite of my flaws. With him, I discovered the true meaning of being loved. What made it a great relationship was that we did not have to force it! It just happened! It was like a puzzle where all of the pieces fit together and just slipped into place. It was so good and so easy. In spite of his cool exterior, he could be so warm and so loving. I became a woman, because for the first time, I had a man!

It makes me smile even now to think about his warm smile, how he was just playful enough to be enjoyed, how my heart ached when I left him, and how it sang for joy when I saw him again. We would cuddle for hours and he was the only man that I've ever known that would invite me over so that we could be alone. We'd be in the same house but different parts, share meals together, and would hug in passing, all while having little interaction or conversation! We were alone together. He was wonderful.

I have this saying on my wall: "Friends are angels who lift us up when we have trouble remembering how to fly!" I don't know who wrote it, because it had no name on it, but I love it! It represents my friends!

When things were not going well for me, I called those days my "I need a hug" days. The people closest to me knew this and were happy to oblige. I learned this from Dell. We shared so much love, and when it was over, I experienced the pain of departure. I felt as if I had been split in half and I did not know how I'd function without him: my other half. I missed him so much. I have never been able to fill the emptiness that he left. I'd lost my best friend and the love of my life all in one day. I only knew that if I survived this, I'd never love this way again. In fact, I don't think that I could ever again. The pain of that loss was too great; the suffering was too long. All I wanted was for it to end. My body simply couldn't take that kind of hurt again.

Since we never lived together, I guess that it made the breakup somewhat easier. I really don't know. I could not imagine it being any harder. At least I did not have to see him every day. I did not have to hear his voice every day, I did not have to smell him every day; all I had to do was miss him forever.

Because of him, I know what love feels like, tastes like, and smells like, and I know how blessed I am to have known real love. Today, I understand it all and I have no regrets! My sister has never known love and has never traveled down that path; I pity anyone who's missed this experience. I only hope to feel it again. When Anita Baker sings, "I want to know what love feels like," I always laughingly say, "Call me, girl, and I'll tell you all about it." I have been blessed to have lived long enough to know what love is as well as the importance of a hug, the value of friendship, and the joys of motherhood. I also am able to see how God works in our lives and am now wise enough to give Him the praise and the glory.

• • •

When one of my sons was a teenager, he had this recurring dream about him and his two uncles. He said that they were about to be nailed to the cross and they were afraid. God spoke to him and said, "Don't be afraid, because I am going to walk you through it so that you will know what to expect. I'll tell you what it's like to have nails driven through your hands and your feet. So, don't be afraid, because I'll be there with you every step of the way."

That was a powerful, powerful dream. Unfortunately, I don't know what others might think, but this is how I explained it to him. I said, "You are someone special because God spoke to you, and God only speaks to those who are not afraid and to those who will hear what He has to say. Something is about to happen in your life and He wants you to know that you don't have to worry and you don't have to be afraid, because He will be there with you every step of the way." I didn't know how to explain his two uncles. I'm still waiting to see what God has in store for him.

At the time, one of his uncles had just come out of the depths of despair and now knows that God had to have been with him. He came out of his situation a "new man" with a new attitude. He now gives God all of the glory and all of the praise. He was made to realize from whence his help comes. He also gives thanks to God because it reaffirmed what daddy had always taught us: the meaning of and value of family. He now knows the importance of both and God.

My other brother, on the other hand, has become somewhat of a skeptic. He knows how good God is, but I think that since he hasn't had a wakeup call in a while, he's just skeptical. Just how my brothers fit into my son's dream, I really don't know, but I do know that I am confident that the message was more about my son than about them. I thank God that He is using my children at a time when so many others have gone astray. My father used to preach to us, "Train up a child in the way he should go, and when he gets older, he will not stray from that." That's what I have tried to do, just as my father did. He was the best living testimony that I know! I just hope that I conveyed that to him while he was alive.

•••

Life has a way of changing things when you finally think that you are on the right track. It can throw a curveball your way that will rock your very core, and that's what happened to us. How much guilt can you feel, how many times can you question yourself about doing things differently, how many tears can you shed, and how many unanswered questions can you have? Throughout this book, I have talked about God and how He hears and answers prayers, but then this happened. I had to ask God if I was asleep. A bigger dagger could not have been put in my heart, and I cannot begin to imagine how his family must have suffered over this. There are just too many questions and too few answers, so I had to turn it over to God, and I am confident still that He will work it out. I have to continue to pray over it.

I have a nephew who spent so much time at my house that I thought (or sometimes felt) that he was my own. We never know when a life-altering thing may happen. As I stated before, we moved away from Texas because my son was advised by the doctor that he needed to be in a better climate. During this time, my older son was in college, and my sister and her husband got a divorce. All of these circumstances sent my nephew's life into a tailspin, and he ended up in trouble. He was an honor student with so much promise and the biggest smile, the best personality, and the biggest heart; he was eager to learn everything. He was a real joy to have around and I loved having him around. He was the brother that my son did not have, and my son was the brother that he didn't have for many years.

Below is a poem that I wrote about that situation. It will give you some explanation as to what happened. It is about someone that I love very deeply. It is a testament to a life that selects you as opposed to one that you elect to have. This poem is dedicated to all the young men and women out there whose lives have taken such a turn, either by choice or necessity. I hope that it will help someone else see that there is help and there is hope. You have to reach out for that help and never give up hope. Together, we can change things, because there are those of us who really care. It is called, "Can He Survive?"

CAN HE SURVIVE?

Wyvonnia Smith-Gorden

I know how he was and how he thought,

But being incarcerated, can he survive or not?

I know what he'd been taught and how he was raised,

But the boys in the hood had him truly amazed.

What will he do and how will he survive

When the boys in the hood have him so hypnotized?

We've been praying and talking, crying and pleading,

But as he stands tall behind the iron bars,

All that we are saying just seems to be seeping.

Straight through his brain and he lets his mouth do the
thinking,

The poor baby doesn't know that his usual smile has
turned to weeping.

What can we do and how can we help?

God only knows as I watched him and wept.

I know there must be something for this poor child

Whose quiet life has suddenly turned bad.

I hear his words and I wonder out loud, "Oh, how sad."

With tears streaming down his little-boy face, the only thing that I can derive:

Can this boy-child, man-child, can he survive?

I know that the Lord up above is still on the throne

As I whisper a prayer, I wonder, *Where did we go wrong?*

He's been such a good child all of his life;

When his parents divorced, his life filled with strife.

About that same time, his surrogate family had to depart.

I guess that it made him wonder, *When is all of this going to stop?*

To further add to the dismantling of his life,

His best friend/cousin left to begin a college life.

Pressure is mounting, and in his family, he's now the new "man,"

Expected to do, function, and be responsible like the head of any clan.

He's just a kid, although tall he may be,

It's a role he cannot handle, and he's afraid that the world will see.

Out in the hood, the pressure is also on

To become "one of them," or, "You won't survive here very long."

The boys in the hood had promised that they'd sell drugs or fight.

The day of reckoning finally came

After the beatings that he and his little brother sustained.

It was evident that things could never be the same.

He had a mother, sister, and a brother that he was now responsible for,

But if he couldn't protect himself or his little brother,

He knew that all alternatives offered lead straight
behind bars.

The question is, and with each and every stride,

Can he, can he, can he survive?

A life where he felt that he no longer fit in,

And how, oh how, can he begin again?

Fate seems to be pushing the odds

And another severe blow has pushed him to the edge.

His new friends are filling all of the voids in his life,

And to family and others, there's now a big wedge.

He's now important, and he's alleviating some strife

For the boys in the hood has given him a rebirth:

A new life, with no school, no family, no plans;

Just hang out and be one of the gang.

And now as I look into those sad, sad eyes,

I watch the tears as they come streaming down.

I have to ask, I have to say,

"Is this the result that is being spread around,

A life filled with nothing but the clang of medal and
the desire to be revived?"

I see his eyes and I hear him speak,

"Whatever the cost, I have to survive! I have to survive!"

As I stated before, my nephew ended up in trouble.
My poem expresses my feelings about his situation. It
is a reflection of the pain, the circumstances, the dis-
appointments, the guilt, the remorse that I personal-
ly went through over this situation. I cannot begin to
imagine what his parents or siblings went through. He
wrote me a poem while he was incarcerated. It is called
"My Day Will Come!"

MY DAY WILL COME

Brian

Even though my days are long and hot

And my nights go by in the blink of an eye,

My body is screaming silent pain that my heart can no
longer ignore.

Although not seen, I feel the foot compressed upon
my back.

I can never condone its ways of torture,

Which are blind to so many of us.

I sit and think, *While in hell,*

Will I ever make it back to heaven again?

My soul is my only bridge that the flames of hell have
not burned.

It will stand 'til the day comes to cross,

But will that day, that day ever come?

Yes! It will come! Our day shall come!

I'm talking about doing whatever to get out of here!

A Letter to My Son

As we all know, kids grow up. As a single parent of boys, I had learned so much from my father. Now I felt compelled to try and pass on some bits of wisdom to one of my sons. Of course, he did not ask for it, but I'm his mother. I'd rather have him hear this from me than someone else. So, I decided to write him this letter (I got his permission to share it here):

Hello my beloved child,

You say that you are in search of "Ms. Right," and no one can be more pleased than I am because I cannot think of anyone more deserving of "Ms. Right" than you. Since this is the first time that you have been close to traveling this road, I thought that I should give you a bit of "fatherly" advice.

Put God first: When I left home, my father said, "Man will disappoint you every time, but God never will!" Don't ever forget this, because things will reach a point in your life where you will definitely understand what this means and just how important this is. You see, we as human beings are imperfect and unreliable, although our intentions may be good. Just don't put all of your faith in man. Find someone who also understands, and...

Love her: Love her with all of your heart! Don't be afraid to say it or to show it! Most importantly, be honest in what you say and in what you do. Love is one of the greatest feelings that you will ever experience, so love with all your heart.

Respect her: Treat her like the "rare find" that you believe she is. If she is not, time will dictate that tale, but it's what and how you feel that is important, because you can only speak for yourself. There might come a time when you feel that she doesn't deserve it, but do it anyway! Always respect her and be worthy of her respect.

Listen to her: Do not talk at her, talk to her! Treat her like the woman you believe her to be. If she hurts, hold her, and if she is happy, laugh with her, and when the world is knocking her down, be her strength and let her know that all of that stops when she's with you. Somebody has to be on her side; even if you think that the matter is silly, listen and show support. Sometimes, saying nothing speaks volumes.

Never hit her: I realize that people are different and that you will disagree, but never allow a disagreement to escalate to the point where you will want to hurt her. If you ever get to that point, walk away! It's not worth it! The ability to walk away can save you lots of hurt and having to take back actions with dire consequences. When you have a diamond, you can't treat it like clay! Always remember that it is a diamond!

Settle arguments: Sit down and talk about whatever it is that is going on with you. Share your feelings and forget the crap about men being the "silent ones," because those men are either living in a dream world, still out there playing with themselves, or trying to buy something that can never be purchased. So, don't make assumptions! Don't get into the mind-reading business, because chances are you will read it wrong. Say what you mean and mean what you say! Don't bully her or try and force your opinion on her. God gave her a mind of her own! Respect that. You cannot make her into what she is not, and it is a waste of time trying! Even if it worked for a short time, in the long run, you will lose.

Be a stand-up man: Don't expect any woman to take care of you! You were raised to be a man, so act the part. Take care of your responsibilities! I realize that a relationship is a partnership, but make sure that both of you understand that from the beginning so that nobody walks away with false expectations. Remember that you cannot raise an adult, you can only be one!

Talk about money/financial issues: The one that is better with money/finances should be the one responsible for it. If she spends recklessly now, she will later. If she has never been taught management skills or if she has some void that she thinks spending will fill, then she is not the one to handle money. Either way, you can't fix it! That's a "Dr. Phil" situation. If you talk about it and you see that it is a bridge that is not worth crossing, leave it alone. It becomes a greater headache later! Operate on a budget; it will pay off later in life. If you make twenty-five cents, try to save at least five cents. It's called "preparing for the future"! Just remember that money ruins many, many relationships!

Talk about wants/expectations: Talk about things that are important to you. Ask what's important to her. For example: does she want children, where would she like to live, does she like travel, etc.? Don't ever allow sex to become a barometer, because that gets old after a while, and then what do you have to fall back on? If you wake up one morning and the sex has disappeared, then what? The best sex that you could possibly have is with someone that you love and respect. Too much emphasis is put on it. Don't allow yourself to be measured by a piece of flesh. You are more than that! Don't ever forget that!

Show compassion: Don't be afraid to say that you hurt when you do! That's a TV kind of thing. You are a human being first and foremost, and you will do what human beings do! Laugh when you are happy, cry when you are sad, and dance when your favorite music is playing. Treat her the same way. Always remember, as you have heard me quote my father many, many times,

"It is easier to live with the consequences of a decision that you have made than it is to live with the consequences of a decision that someone else made for you." So, don't be afraid to make a decision; someone has to! As the Bible says in James 1:19 (KJV), "Wherefore, my beloved brethren, let every man be swift to hear, slow to speak, slow to wrath:"

Now, if you have done all that you could possibly have done and things still do not work out, just remember: don't be mad because she left, be extremely happy that she came! When you think of her, smile, remember all of the good times, and know that something better is coming your way. You realize that we make decisions and God makes decisions, and if it is not a "God" decision, it's not going to work, anyway! So, relish the fact that you had great times and know that more are forthcoming. I don't know what men say to their male children, but I know the kind of men that I want my male children to be, and it's what I have written here. I know that it is not a perfect formula, but I believe with all of my heart that it is a winning one.

Love ya,
Mom

Life Lessons
(From My Perspective)

1. Never expect anyone to love you more than you love yourself.

2. Being a wonderful person does not mean being a perfect person.

3. It is easier to live with the consequences of a decision that you made than one your friends or relatives made for you.

4. Sex does not mean love.

5. Talk less and listen more.

6. Never have sex with someone who cannot afford child support or who you consider to be unattractive, because they could produce your future children.

7. It is just as easy to hook up with someone who is uneducated, unemployed, and has no sense of

direction as it is to hook up with someone who is not all of those things. Consider that when you think of marriage; it will prove to be important.

8. Beware of people who are constantly putting you down. They are only using you to build themselves up.

9. Expensive clothes do not make you beautiful. Beauty shines from within.

10. Only you can decide your worth. Don't allow anyone else to dictate your value. You deserve the very best that life has to offer.

11. You must respect yourself if you expect others to respect you.

12. Be a decision-maker; don't allow others to make your decisions. If someone else is involved, it must be a mutual decision.

13. Cherish love, because it doesn't come your way every day.

14. Keep God foremost in your life. He understands when no one else does.

15. Treat family with love and respect, because they will be there when everyone else walks away.

16. Give freely from the heart without strings and attachments.

17. Remember that nobody owes you anything.

18. Be kind and kindness will be returned to you.

19. Be the kind of friend that you want, not necessarily the kind of friend that you have.

20. Love with all you have, because nothing feels better, but if it ends, cry and let it go. Don't be sad because it is over, just be thankful that you had the experience. So many people go through life never having known this feeling.

21. Remember that it is just as easy to make friends as it is to make enemies. True friends last a lifetime; others are in your life for reason or for a season.

22. Pray for what you want. Be specific in your request, because God gives us what we need, not necessarily what we want. Remember that He knows what is best for you.

23. When you are older, reflect on unanswered prayers and give thanks to God for being so much wiser than you were at the time.

24. If you like no one else, like the person that you see in the mirror. Examine what you see daily, and the things that you do not like—change them.

Always remember that I only want the best for you.

Love,
Mom

Epilogue

My elder son did well in elementary and high school in spite of the previous threat of impending blindness. He was an honor student throughout. He often represented the school on different occasions in all kinds of academics. When he graduated from the High School for Health Professions, he was given the Adams Award. This award is only given to a select student, and he was the one! Because only one student is awarded this, he never had a clue that he was being considered. It shows that others had the same belief in his becoming a medical doctor as I did. The inscription reads:

> "In the spirit of the prototypic American country doctor, this award ispresented to you in hopes that the recipient will keep this people-oriented tradition alive."

After high school, my older son set his sights on Creighton University in Omaha, Nebraska; he was offered a full scholarship and was convinced that that was his calling. I, on the other hand, knew better, but I kept my opinion to myself. I just reminded him that where God wants you to be is where you are supposed to be. So, that summer, he was selected for an internship program at Texas A&M, and that is where he spent the next four years of his college life. He called me one day and said, "Mom, this is where I am supposed to be!" I just smiled, because I already knew.

Many wonderful things happened at Texas A&M. For example, he had been chosen to tutor students on many different occasions. He was a biochemistry major and was a good student. Usually, when asked to tutor, he would be given a grade or compensation for his work. On this occasion, he was not offered either. There would be no compensation at all. He never argued about it, but was a bit disappointed, as he was the child of a single parent who was also low income. He did his very best and the students excelled. When it was over, the professor went to him and praised him for a job well done. He was happy then, because at least his work had been acknowledged. This professor later went on to offer him a fellowship to do biochemical research in Switzerland. He was flabbergasted, but said yes. He would have to pay for his trip and be reimbursed when the year was over. The professor asked if he could pay for his trip, and he again said yes. He told me that he had been recommended because he had proven that he was good at what he did. He never questioned God, we simply prayed, and when he got on the plane to go to Switzerland, his ticket was paid for and he had money in his pockets, plus suitable clothes for the cold weather there! Isn't God good?

Prior to going to Switzerland, my son had selected seven medical schools that were of interest to him and was granted interviews at *all* seven! This included Duke, Emory, and Harvard. Prior to leaving for Switzerland, he had underestimated the time and cost and did not realize how time-consuming it would be to go back and forth across the country to interview, so he couldn't make all of his interviews. He called and informed them that he had to leave for Switzerland and would be unable to interview until after his return.

However, that was not good enough for Stanford University, because acceptance dates would have passed, and they really wanted him there. They wanted to know who he had already interviewed with, so I told them. They then wanted to know how to contact him in Switzerland, and I gave them his address. Days went by, and they informed me that they had gotten him to sign a release for Harvard to give them a copy of his interview. The people at Harvard were not too happy about that. Stanford offered him a place upon his return from Switzerland, and he became the first student to ever enter Stanford University School of Medicine without a personal interview. Ironically enough, he later became a resident at Harvard's Boston Children's Hospital after he graduated and worked there for years. Today, he is Chief of Newborn Medicine at Boston Medical. Only God knows where he will go from there, but wherever it is, we know that it will be the *right* place for him! Isn't God good?

My younger son was an honor student in high school, received the Intellect Award, scored extremely high on the SAT, and was honored by the governor. He was offered a scholarship to Duke but opted to follow in his uncle's footsteps and attended Morehouse College, where he graduated Phi Beta Kappa. He also participated in all kinds of academics in school. He now lives and works in Washington, DC. Life has been good, and my two sons are my blessings to show just how good God is!

Keep away from people who try to belittle your ambitions. Small people always do that, but the really great people make you feel that you, too, can become great.

Mark Twain

A Father's Love

FRANK-ISMS

I was encouraged to write this book and I did not understand why. Finally, my older son said that I needed to share those Frank-isms with someone other than my children. I guess that I did not realize how I had pounded them into my children as my father had pounded them into me. Not only did he tell us these things, but he lived them in front of us every day. I hated hearing them growing up, but after growing up and becoming a parent myself, I knew the value of them:

1. God doesn't walk away from us; we walk away from Him.

2. Vote! People died for this right.

3. It is a poor man that does not rule his own house.

4. It is easier to live with a decision that you make

than one that someone else makes for you.

5. Don't let anyone disrespect your wife. Your husband should be able to take care of himself.

6. Be careful who you hang out with, and don't hang out with people that you can't take home with you.

7. Keep God first and foremost in your life and everything else will fall into place.

8. Stand up for what you believe in because everyone should believe in and stand up for something.

9. Get as much education as you can, because people can take a lot of things away from you, but they can never take your brains.

10. Be on time!

11. Help other people; the world is bigger than you are.

12. Take pride in what you do regardless of what it is.

13. Respect others and what belongs to them.

14. Stay out of trouble.

15. If you go to jail for something that you did not do,

I will fight until the end to get you set free.

16. If you go to jail for something that you were stupid enough to do, I'll help them prosecute you.

17. Raise your children in the church. They won't understand it while they are young, but when they grow up, they will appreciate you for it.

18. Your word should be your bond. If your word is no good, then neither are you.

19. Leave what belongs to others alone; if they want you to have it, they will give it to you.

20. Wear comfortable shoes. You'll appreciate it when you get older.

21. Take pride in how you live and in how you look: you never know who's watching.

22. Don't run from a fight. If so, you will have to keep on running.

23. Don't try to fix other people, just fix you.

24. Don't lay in the bed all day, get up and out of the house, because there is plenty to see and do. You

can rest when you can't do anything else.

25. Don't argue with a fool! You know that they are a fool, so why waste your time?

26. Persevere: quitters don't win anything, not even the satisfaction of having tried.

27. Keep family first, but be there for others.

28. There are no classes on being a parent, and if you don't like what I'm doing as a parent, don't pass it on to your children! Throw it out and only pass on what you feel that I did right.

29. Pay your bills on time, and if you don't have money, you can still get what you want because your credit is good.

30. A man takes care of his family. If you happen to be a woman without a husband, then you take care of your family.

31. Don't settle for just anything, because you deserve the best!

32. Always pray for guidance. God hears and answers prayers. When you pray with a sincere heart, He

knows, so don't play around with Him.

33. When you graduate from high school, you must get out! You have no reason to stay around here. The world is a big place.

34. Take care of yourself; don't ever rely on someone else to take care of you. Be independent!

35. Don't lay with a man that is not qualified to be a father and who won't be able to take care of his kids. You will appreciate it later.

36. Don't bother anybody, but give them hell if they bother you!

I have many faults, but no regrets! The Lord used my mistakes to build my character and to strengthen my faith!

Unknown

WHAT IS A FATHER?

Wyvonnia Smith-Gorden

A father is a man whose life is spent working hard
each and every day

Tending to the family's needs and brightening their
way

By sharing and caring and sacrificing too

In working out problems and making dreams come
true.

A Father is a man who smooths the road for his kids
to follow after,

He helps to make the home a place

Of cheer, fun, and laughter.

Seldom does he get the praise that he's sure to rate;

His family is his number one priority

And they think that he's absolutely great!

He puts his family's needs above his own;

He provides love, care, and can hold his own.

He's not jealous or possessive,

But a caring man

Who knows the importance of following God's plan.

His shoes are too big for just anyone to fill;

He takes his role seriously and "for real."

He keeps his priorities intact;

He never forgets whose he is, and that's a fact.

He's loving and kind and always listens,

Gives good advice and knows what seems to be missing.

In other words, he really understands,

Because my father is one big, big man!

I know that there were days when he wanted to quit.

Because of the love for his family,

He never gave up:

He held on, he did not quit!

He knew that all of the challenges

Were there for a reason,

So he held on knowing that

This was simply a season.

Life may not have always been

Everything that he wanted it to be,

But thank God that he never gave up on me.

So, all and all,

This is a father to me:

One who stands strong, tall, and who perseveres,

One who loves and protects kids like me.

ABOUT THE AUTHOR

Wyvonnia Smith-Gorden grew up in rural Georgia on a peach plantation as the seventh child in a family of ten children. Her father, a long-distance truck driver, was the ruler of the house even when he was absent. Despite her annoyance with them as a child, his "Frank-isms" still apply to her life today, and she is now thankful for everything he taught her. Wyvonnia realized that because of those prayer services that her father made her listen to as a child (despite pretending to be asleep so that she would not be asked to join in) made a difference in her life and that of her children.

His goodness is shining so brightly through my window right now.

Iris Farmer

Thank you and blessings to you!